MEXICO 1968

A Diary of the XIXth Olyn

BOOKS BY CHRISTOPHER BRASHER

The Red Snow (with Sir John Hunt)
Sportsmen of Our Time
Tokyo 1964—A Diary of the XVIIIth Olympiad

MEXICO 1968

A Diary of the XIXth Olympiad

CHRISTOPHER BRASHER

 STANLEY PAUL London

STANLEY PAUL & CO LTD
178–202 Great Portland Street, London W1

AN IMPRINT OF THE HUTCHINSON GROUP

London Melbourne Sydney
Auckland Bombay Toronto
Johannesburg New York

First published 1968

© Christopher Brasher 1968

*This book has been set in Plantin, printed in Great Britain
on Antique Wove paper by Anchor Press, and
bound by Wm. Brendon, both of Tiptree, Essex*

09 096830 1

This book is dedicated to the British Olympic Team – not quite so successful a team as that which came back from Tokyo in 1964 but nevertheless the second most successful Olympic team since the war.

THE MEDALLISTS

GOLD

    David Hemery   (400 metres Hurdles)
    Robert Braithwaite   (Clay Pigeon Shooting)
    Rodney Pattisson
    Iain Macdonald-Smith   (Flying Dutchman)

    Major Derek Allhusen
    Staff-Sergeant Ben Jones
    Richard Meade   (Three Day Event)
    Jane Bullen

    Christopher Finnegan   (Boxing)

SILVER

    Sheila Sherwood   (Long Jump)
    Lillian Board   (400 metres)
    Marion Coakes   (Show Jumping)
    Martyn Woodroffe   (200 metres Butterfly)
    Major Derek Allhusen   (Three Day Event)

BRONZE

    John Sherwood   (400 metres Hurdles)

    Robin Aisher
    Paul Anderson   (5.5 metres)
    Adrian Jardine

    David Broome   (Show Jumping)

M.—A*

CONTENTS

1	'There will be those who will die'	1
2	'Three ruddy hundredths of a second'	11
3	'Only the British would be gentlemen'	24
4	'We are fighting for Mexico'	29
5	'Fear is the greatest spur'	35
6	The opening	40
7	'In fair and equal competition'	43
8	'You are happy just to be in the final'	49
9	'There are a thousand hills and sand-dunes behind you . . .'	57
10	'If I do something good then I am an American, but if I do something bad then I am a Negro'	69
11	'Oh God, it's over'	75
12	'I can't go on. What is the point'	81
13	'Please stand by me in my hour of need'	86
14	The Fosbury flop—'It's meditation'	90
15	'Damn the jury. We'll show them now'	97
16	'Concentration is the quality that makes champions'	102
17	'I'm not just a silly old bricklayer' by Hugh McIlvanney	107
18	The end of a love affair	116
19	Farewell	123
	Mexico 1968 results	124

ILLUSTRATIONS

Between pages 50 and 51

1 The members and officials of the British Olympic team during the opening ceremonies
2 Enriqueta Basilo carries the Olympic torch
3 Sheila Sherwood wins Great Britain's first medal
4 David Hemery on his way to victory in the 400 metres hurdles
5 Jim Hines wins the final of the 100 metres
6 David Hemery waves at the crowd after receiving his gold medal
7 Randy Matson in action
8 The Netherlands men's team *en route* to victory in the 100 kilometres time-trial
9 Tommie Smith wins the 200 metres
10 Bob Seagren clears the bar in the pole vault
11 Lillian Board comes in second in the 400 metres
12 The field in the 50 kilometres walk
13 Willie Davenport finishes the 110 metres hurdles
14 Yanis Lusis wins the gold medal in the javelin
15 Bob Beamon's world record jump of 29 ft $2\frac{1}{2}$ in.
16 Gyula Zsivotsky sets a new Olympic record in the hammer

17 'The Fosbury Flop'
18 Kipchoge Keino wins the 1500 metres final
19 Jim Hines in the 4 × 100 metres relay
20 *Superdocious*, winner of the Flying Dutchman class
21 Great Britain's victorious equestrian team
22 Debbie Meyer wins the women's 200 metres free-style final
23 Lajos Szucs scores Hungary's fifth goal
24 Ingeborg Busch dives from the highboard
25 Felipe Munoz wins Mexico's first gold medal
26 Marion Coakes on Stroller wins a silver medal
27 Yugoslavia wins the basketball semi-final against U.S.S.R.
28 Jean Allemand tumbles off the platform during the épée finals
29 Sharon Wichman of United States on her way to a gold medal
30 Tibor Tatai of Hungary wins the Canadian Singles canoe race
31 Christopher Finnegan is awarded his gold medal

1
'THERE WILL BE THOSE WHO WILL DIE'

Take six princes, one marquis, two counts, three barons, five generals, one rajah, two sheiks, a sprinkling of millionaires and a comrade or two. Place them in a casino in a watering spa overlooked by turreted castles and the stage is set for a Ruritanian farce. At any moment Peter Ustinov, in white knee-breeches and gold-encrusted blue tunic, will march on stage and the action will begin.

But this is no fantasy. This is a full meeting of the International Olympic Committee, gathered in the town of Baden-Baden, West Germany, in October 1963.

I, like many other journalists, was in Baden-Baden that sunny week to report on the fate of South Africa. A year before, at their meeting in Moscow, the I.O.C. had delivered an ultimatum to the South African Olympic Committee requiring them to honour clause one of the Fundamental Principles of the Olympic Games: 'No discrimination is allowed against any country or person on grounds of race, religion or political affiliation.'

Despite the ultimatum, no clear-cut decision was made and the South African affair went simmering on for another five years. But at that meeting in Baden-Baden, with the roulette wheels clicking in the plush casino below the conference chamber, the International Olympic Committee did take one decision the significance of which escaped me—and all the other journalists. They chose Mexico City as the site of the 19th Olympic Games.

A year later Abebe Bikila, the great Ethiopian marathon runner, the man who had come padding up the Via Appia in Rome to win the 1960 marathon and then had repeated his feat in Tokyo, held a press conference under the concrete stands of the Olympic Stadium in Tokyo. He was asked whether he would compete in Mexico City and try for the hat-trick. 'Yes,' he said, 'and I will win. Mexico City is at the same height as Addis Ababa.'

A day or two later I visited the Ethiopian headquarters in the Olympic village and talked to Onni Niskanen, the Swedish physical educationalist, Bikila's coach and a man who had spent eighteen years in Addis Ababa. He said quietly: 'An Olympic athlete will always do his utmost, but few of them will have any idea of what the lack of oxygen can do to those who are not used to altitude. Suddenly—blackout. There will be those who will die.'

Those words echoed round the world and started the whole furore. I think it is no exaggeration to say that millions of words have been written about the effect of altitude on athletic performances since Onni Niskanen made his pronouncement. And yet there is still tremendous ignorance. Only a week ago, on returning from Mexico, I was confronted with a letter from the Press Secretary of the Mexican Embassy in London in which she complained gently to the editor of the *Observer* about the tone of our reporting from the Games. In her letter she said that the number of records broken during the Games proved that altitude was no disadvantage! I have known people twist the facts before but it is beyond my belief that after all that has been written and said in these past four years anyone could still fail to realise that altitude was a decisive factor in Mexico and that it made the 19th Games the 'Unfair Games'.

So, because the question of altitude is going to affect everything I write in these next pages, let us try to clarify the position once and for all. The first and most salient fact is that Mexico City lies at an altitude of 7347 feet above sea-level. The higher you go above sea-level, the thinner becomes the air. Eventually when man reaches the summit of Everest, just over 29,000 feet, the air is so thin that he cannot walk even one step without taking two deep breaths. This phenomenon produces different effects on those who take part in events which only take a few seconds and those who compete in events which depend on the efficient use of oxygen by the body.

Bear with me if I go back to what I said about this problem

when I first raised it in the *Observer* in 1965. I am not trying to prove how clever we were to raise it on such an early date, but I am trying to show that the basic principles of the problem could easily be detected in 1965 and that there was no reason why the International Olympic Committee could not have done a little homework in 1963 at Baden-Baden before awarding the games to Mexico City:

'I cannot pretend to be an authority on the medical aspects of high-altitude competition, but what is established beyond doubt is that athletes in the explosive events (sprints, shot putt, etc.) can significantly improve their performances because of the reduced atmospheric pressure (27 per cent less at 7500 feet than at sea-level) and reduced air density (23 per cent less at 7500 feet than at sea-level).

'So performances in the explosive events will be phenomenal—almost every world record will tumble, not because the athletes are necessarily any faster or stronger than their predecessors but just because the air density is so reduced. (All the horse-racing sprint records—from 2 furlongs to $3\frac{1}{2}$ furlongs—were established in Mexico City!) Surely records established in such conditions are farcical.

'Conversely, all the distance events will be run in excruciatingly slow times with a danger that some athletes will collapse. Those people who saw the Jim Peters incident at the Commonwealth Games in Vancouver in 1954 will know what a ghastly sight it is to see a man driving himself beyond the limits of his body. But what is even more important is that an athlete can suffer permanent damage if he drives himself beyond the limit in artificial conditions—and what athlete doesn't drive himself to the limit in the Olympic Games? In Vancouver it was the heat that affected Peters. In Mexico City it will be the oxygen deficiency that will affect the athletes.

'My opinion on such a matter may not carry much weight, but Dr. Roger Bannister's certainly does, and he has told me he does not consider it justified to hold the endurance events in Mexico City. He does not go nearly as far as Onni Niskanen. He does not say, "There will be those that will die". But he does believe that there is the possibility that someone may be permanently affected. Surely the I.O.C. cannot take such a risk.

'Of course, much can be done to acclimatise an athlete to high altitude, but only at the expense of considerable time. A man who has lived all his life at over 7000 feet will be far better acclimatised than someone who has spent only a month at this altitude. This is why it is a safe bet that, barring accidents, Abebe Bikila will win the marathon for the third successive Olympics—an unparalleled feat.

'It is on this question of the time taken to acclimatise that I base the weight of my argument. To hold the endurance events in Mexico City is to commit what I will call "an offence against the spirit of the Olympic Games".

'For years the International Olympic Committee has fought against professionalism in the Games. There are two aspects to professionalism—money and time. It is fairly easy to ensure that no one who has competed for money is allowed to take part in the Olympics. It is much more difficult to eliminate what I call "the time professionals"—or in other words the people who have no job or career but who are supported in some way that enables them to devote all their time and energy to their chosen sport.

'Up to now this has not been a serious problem. It has always been possible for a man who is prepared to devote two hours a day to his training to compete on equal terms with a "time professional". In fact he often has an advantage in that he is mentally much fresher. But if the Olympic endurance events are to be held in Mexico City then the "time professional" will have an immense advantage. Even if it is decided that the British Olympic team should go to Mexico City one month before the Games (and this means in effect that they will have to get about two months' leave of absence from their jobs) they will be at a great disadvantage to the athletes who have four to six months to train and acclimatise at a high altitude.

'One can confidently predict that the Americans and the Russians will take their teams to training camps at high altitudes and keep them there for months on end. Other countries which give a considerable amount of State aid to sport will no doubt do the same.

'And that to me is complete and utter professionalism. For the first time in the history of the modern Olympics it will be possible to "buy" an Olympic medal.'

I, and many others, then started a campaign to try to get the venue for the distance events changed to a new location that would be fair to everyone and which would eliminate any danger to athletes' health. But there did not seem to be much chance of this. The Marquis of Exeter, who has a triple role in the Olympics as a member of the International Olympic Committee, President of the International Amateur Athletic Federation (the body which controls all the track and field events at the Olympics) and Chairman of the British Olympic Association, said: 'The Olympics have been allocated to Mexico City and there is no question of any change.'

He went on to emphasise that there were no facts to support a case for a change and one reluctantly had to agree with him. Very few world-class athletes had ever competed at such altitudes and we were having to rely largely on theory. What really worried me was that nobody would have any hard facts until it was too late for the venue to be changed.

In the last months of 1965 the British Olympic Association sent out a research team of six distance athletes, together with a coach and two doctors, including Dr. Griffith Pugh, a physiologist who works for the Medical Research Council, a noted skier and a mountaineer who was a member of the successful Everest expedition in 1953.

One of the distance athletes who took part in these trials was Martin Hyman, one-time holder of the British six-mile record and a man who had always applied his brain to his running. On his return he said: 'If I had my heart set on an Olympic medal I would give up my job one year before the Games and take another one at a similar altitude to Mexico City. With the present state of knowledge about acclimatisation it would be risky to take less than nine months. Even with one year's acclimatisation at 7500 feet there is a possibility that you might be beaten by someone who had been acclimatised at a higher altitude.'

My comment at the time (January 1966) was: 'There are two tragi-comic situations. First we have the athletes, leap-frogging over one another, trying to discover the optimum height which will give them the maximum acclimatisation and yet still allow them to train hard.

'Secondly, we have the spectacle of Avery Brundage (President of the International Olympic Committee) and the Marquis of Exeter standing on a seashore at the bottom of a valley, trying to turn the tide of professionalism (in its accepted sense of those who take money for their sport) and not knowing that a dam has burst behind them and let out a flood of far more dangerous professionalism.

'They do not seem to have realised that the real danger to the ideals of the Olympics comes from those who forsake a normal career in order to devote themselves full-time to the pursuit of a gold-plated medal.

'Up to now these time professionals have had little advantage over those who have trained and worked, for it is the intensity of training rather than the duration which really counts. But in Mexico City no distance athlete, however naturally gifted, will be able to compete on an equal footing with someone who has devoted himself to the problem of acclimatisation.

'The proof of this lies in these figures, all of which are the average of six athletes' times in a three-mile race:

'England:
        During October: 13 min 36.5 sec

Mexico City:
        After 8 days: 14 min 48.3 sec
        After 16 days: 14 min 39.5 sec
        After 24 days: 14 min 36.2 sec
        After 32 days: 14 min 29.2 sec

'For the moment let us forget the huge differential between England and Mexico, and concentrate on the improvement as acclimatisation progresses. Between weeks one and two it is 8.8 sec, between weeks two and three it is 3.3 sec and between weeks three and four it is 7 sec. Now seven seconds over three miles is a very considerable margin. Applied to the equivalent Olympic event in Tokyo (the 5000 metres) seven seconds is the difference between a gold medal and an unsung eighth place.

'A seven-second improvement in terms of training means night after night of thudding around the roads with sweat staining the white vest one wears to save one from being run down by a motorist on his way home to supper and a fire. How many nights of training? Impossible to say, but certainly measured in terms of months rather than days.

'So, in 1968, an athlete will not be worrying so much about whether he's done enough training but about how long he has been able to acclimatise.

'The six British athletes in Mexico City were still acclimatising at the end of a month, although the speed of their acclimatisation was falling off. But still the evidence shows that the longer you spend at altitudes the faster you run.

'There is no real evidence about the long-term improvement, but let us be conservative and say that the improvement between the fifth and sixth months would be only about two seconds. This is still a very significant margin in the Olympics. Again, taking the Tokyo 5000 metres as an example, it is the difference between a gold medal and sixth place.

'It means that those athletes who are supported by a massive research team and who have the freedom of movement and time to experiment, are going to have an immeasurable advantage over the athletes who train normally at home and then go to Mexico for four weeks' acclimatisation before the Games. I don't know what this might be called, but it is certainly not sport.

'Apparently we are lumbered with Mexico City as the site of the 1968 Games. The International Olympic Committee have made a ghastly mistake and there is, so they say, no going back on the decision. So athletes who still have some pretensions to a medal in 1968 and who cannot afford to throw up their jobs might like to ponder two points.

'There is some evidence, inconclusive at the moment, that an athlete may be able to cut down on his acclimatisation period if he goes to a greater height than 7500 feet. The only snag is that the higher you go, the more difficult it becomes to carry out a normal training programme. Nobody has yet been able to work out an equation based on height, speed of acclimatisation and work done. And even if they did it would probably have to be modified for each individual.

'The second point is one that I would recommend to British athletes who still have a job to do. Himalayan mountaineering experience tends to show that acclimatisation is quicker on the second and third trip to a height, and although this is imprecise information, it is supported by some evidence which I have recently received from Peru.

'It may, therefore, be a good idea for an athlete to spend his holidays between now and 1968 training at a high altitude.

'The whole situation is beginning to border on farce. It is ceasing to be sport and beginning to resemble the space race, where the astronaut's first duty on descending is to report to the medicine men.'

That was the state of our knowledge in January 1966. It produced great depression—even fear—amongst some British middle- and long-distance athletes. It even worried some of the short-distance men and women who had not yet realised that the opportunity of competing at altitude against top-class athletes was going to give them the chance of recording performances that they had never dreamt of before.

What was needed now was an opportunity for the potential British Olympic team to train and compete at altitude so that they could discover for themselves what it was really like. In November 1966 the Sports Council gave them that opportunity.

Walter Winterbottom, the Director of the Council, wrote to all the governing bodies of the Olympic sports to say that arrangements had been made with the French authorities so that British athletes could make use of the newly built high-altitude training centre at Font Romeu in the Pyrenees. The response was pitiful. Out of the nineteen Olympic sports, only the athletes, fencers and modern 'pentathletes' showed any interest.

Walter Winterbottom and his chief, Denis Howell, the Minister for Sport, convinced of the necessity for our men and women to get altitude experience, wrote again six months later, asking all the governing bodies to state their definite requirements for altitude training and also extending to them the invitation from the Mexican organising committee to attend the 'Little Olympics' in Mexico City in October 1967. It is worth recording that the first people to reply were the yachtsmen—and they had not even got an altitude problem because the yachting events were to be held on the Pacific coast in the resort of Acapulco.

They intended to go to Mexico in October 1967 to gain experience of the winds and tides in Acapulco Bay. I wrote at the time: 'No altitude problem here, just the wise precaution of gaining experience. Britain's only gold medal in 1952 was won by a horse. Perhaps the only gold medal of 1968 will be won by a yacht!'

This was an attitude that I liked—a professional attitude. I do not use the word 'professional' in the sense of one who is paid for his sport but in the sense that here is someone with a belief in his sport who is going to apply his brains to becoming good at it. The athletes were to have a long struggle with their amateur administrators before they were to achieve a similar approach—and then they only got it because they took matters into their own hands.

The athletes now have their own 'union' (the International Athletes Club) and it was this club which approached the *Daily Mirror* to raise money for altitude training. The *Mirror* generously gave £2000 and at the end of August 1967 a team of nearly forty athletes set out for Font Romeu to spend ten days finding out just what effect altitude was to have on their performances. They had great fun and they discovered many things—principally the fact that the really fit athlete need have no fears of altitude provided he abided by a few simple rules. But, of course, it was only a taste of the problems, only the *hors-d'œuvre* before the meal of 1968.

I began to feel much more hopeful about the prospects in Mexico. I began, indeed, to get angry at the attitude of some distance runners who still believed that the situation was hopeless. Altitude would affect everyone, even those born and bred on the heights, and if only the sea-level men could get enough experience, and apply some of the research of men like Griff Pugh, then there was still hope. Class, that indefinable quality that lifts an athlete into world class, would surely tell, and there were some class athletes in the British team.

Of course, they needed more experience at altitude and few of them would be able to afford the time. And then there was also that restriction imposed by the International Olympic Committee in 1966. The Committee, worried at the proliferation of high-altitude training camps and at the advantage that their choice of Mexico City would confer on the full-time professional, had passed a rule, which said: 'In regard to the coming Olympic Games in Mexico City, the I.O.C. has decided that to achieve fairness as far as possible between competitors, no athlete, other than those who usually live and train at such heights, shall specially do so at high altitudes for more than four weeks in the last three months before the opening of the Games. The I.O.C. points out that to break this rule would be a gross breach of good sportsmanship and is sure that no one connected with the Olympic movement would wish in any way to be guilty of taking an unfair advantage over the other competitors.'

Of course, the British would abide by this rule for it was passed at the instigation of the Marquis of Exeter, himself British, himself an Olympic gold medallist.

The British plans were to spend the four weeks allowed in Mexico City before the Games opened and this would mean that the only other opportunity of high-altitude training would be in the early months of 1968 before the I.O.C.'s rule became effective on July 12th, 1968.

With all the difficulties of athletes obtaining time off from their work there could only be one other high-altitude training session —a brief ten days, also at Font Romeu, in May 1968. Not so for the other nations. Many of them, as we shall see later, blatantly disregarded the I.O.C. rule in their quest for medals in Mexico.

But before we investigate one such example of cheating it is time to turn to the celebration of the winter games in Grenoble, France.

2
'THREE RUDDY HUNDREDTHS OF A SECOND'

'Three ruddy hundredths of a second.' This may not be a very ladylike remark but it was entirely appropriate to the occasion—the finish of the ladies slalom at the Winter Olympics in Grenoble, France, in February 1968. It came from Gina Hathorn, a round-faced twenty-one-year-old skier from Hampshire, just after she failed, by the incredibly small margin of three hundredths of a second, to become the first British girl to win an Olympic skiing medal.

To appreciate Miss Hathorn's feat, let me explain that no competition from a lowland country has won a medal in the Alpine ski events—centrepiece of the Winter Olympic Games—for as long as anyone can remember.

Skiing is a national sport in the European Alpine countries and a mammoth industry in both the United States and Canada. None of the competitors from these countries expects a Britisher to invade their preserves any more than we expect any of these countries to invade the cricket scene.

The slalom is the event in skiing which requires the greatest technique. The course is not very long, not much more than two or three hundred yards, but in this distance the skier has to negotiate some forty or fifty 'gates' which are placed at the most awkward angles so that the skier is constantly having to twist and turn. The winner in Grenoble was Marielle Goitschel of France, one of the two skiing sisters who came from the lovely French skiing resort of Val d'Isère. Miss Goitschel, the silver medallist in the 1964 Olympics at Innsbruck (where the slalom title went to her sister Christine), won in a time of 1 min 25.86 sec. The silver medal was won by pretty Nancy Greene of Canada in a time of 1 min 26.15 sec, and the bronze medal was won by Annie Famose, also of France, in a time of 1 min 27.89 sec. Gina Hathorn's time, in fourth place, was 1 min 27.92 sec, and only the electrical timing mechanism could separate these two.

So how does it happen that a British girl can become the fourth-best slalom skier in the world? Like all Olympic medals it has been done by hard work and enthusiasm. 'There are no miracles in skiing,' says charming Maria Goldberger, manager of the British women's skiing team. 'Just four years of concentrated effort.'

Gina Hathorn is too fit to be chubby, but she is distinctly, and delightfully, pneumatic. She wears her hair drawn back into a pony-tail, which makes her face look rounder than it is, and she worries about her weight, saying that once she has finished with skiing she really is going to slim.

The breakthrough for her, and for the British ladies team, came in 1966 when the world championships were held in Chile in the northern summer. 'For the first time our girls had a chance of skiing throughout the year, like the Continentals,' says Mrs. Goldberger. That winter Miss Hathorn came second in a slalom in Grindelwald against the best skiers in the world. Now even the French pronounce her name correctly.

To be well off enough to ski for eighteen months out of twenty-four, as these British girls have done since 1966, may sound like the perfect life, but there is nothing dilettante about any of them. Mrs. Goldberger started their preparations six months ago, in August, with two weeks in Cervinia on the Italian side of the Matterhorn. They skied in the morning on the slopes above the Theodule Pass and then ran downhill (without their skis) in the afternoon.

Then they went to France for ten days' conditioning training under Honoré Bonnet, the French ski team's trainer—gym work, interval training through the woods, weight training with light weights, and balance and relaxation—a type of yoga—under a Monsieur Coulon, a French trainer who has managed to do wonders with the great French skier Jean Claude Killy.

To help them with this fitness training the British girls took their bicycles as well—small-wheeled Moultons. But they were too embarrassed to join in with the French girls who had donned their full Tour de France cycling rig and climbed on to their individually tailored, featherweight racing machines for a quick forty- or fifty-mile ride over a few Alpine passes.

Then in October, five months before the Games, they undertook three more weeks' conditioning training at the Crystal Palace Recreational Centre under John Salisbury, the 1958 European 400 metres champion. Then they started skiing in earnest in November, four months before the Games.

Mrs. Goldberger believes it is this conditioning training which has helped put the British girls on a par with the best Continentals. 'When all the training was done on snow, we just couldn't compete because we couldn't afford to spend all our time there. But now there is such a vogue for this basic fitness we can do it just as well in England as anywhere else.'

Gina Hathorn was not the only star of this small British women's team. Divina Galica, who at twenty-three is two years older than Miss Hathorn, was also expected to do well, but this time in the women's downhill course—a ferocious descent, over a mile long, which scared me into a trembling wreck when I tried to ski it before the Games opened.

The weather on the day of the women's downhill race was very strange. Overcast and dull in Grenoble, misty on the road up to Chamrousse, the ski resort some ten miles outside Grenoble where all the Alpine events were held. It was a tricky morning for the trainers of the teams. The start was at twelve o'clock and throughout the morning the sun grew in power, chasing away the mist and cloud.

The British trainer, Gaston Perrot, a handsome Frenchman from Chamonix, took the temperature of the snow on the one-and-a-third-mile-long run very early in the morning and found it to be very cold indeed. So he waxed the girls' skis for cold conditions—and thereby hangs the tale of the women's downhill, for it was a race won partly on sheer technical knowledge.

Those who waxed correctly, those who had team officials dotted down the course and walkie-talkie radios with which to relay information back to the start, came through. Those who didn't, ploughed through the soft, warm snow to finish amongst the also-rans.

The favourite for the women's downhill was perky Nancy Greene, of Canada, the winner of the Ladies' World Cup in 1967. She started early—fifth girl down—and this is important, for it was the early starters who realised that their wax was wrong. Her time was 1 min 43.12 sec—competent but not great. Seconds after she had crossed the finishing line she was skating uphill on her skis to grab a walkie-talkie and warn her team-mates who were waiting to start that the course was now slow and that the snow was warm.

Divina Galica did not know about the condition of the course when her turn (number 12) came. As she went down the first gentle slope, working and pushing, trainer Perrot realised his mistake. Quickly he changed the wax on the other girls' skis, but the damage was done for Divina—and Perrot was near to tears.

The early competitors—who achieved their start placings because they had proved themselves in previous races to be the best—usually have the advantage, for they run on the prepared piste before it starts to rut. However, on this occasion it was the later starters who had the advantage.

Olga Pall, a chunky twenty-year-old petrol-pump attendant, started fifteenth and finished first for the gold medal in a time of 1 min 40.87 sec. Isabelle Mir, an eighteen-year-old French girl, started thirteenth and won the silver medal with the time of 1 min 41.33 sec. The best British performance came from Felicity 'Bunny' Field, a well-built twenty-one-year-old who bubbles with enthusiasm. She started twenty-first and finished sixth in 1 min 42.79 sec, less than $1\frac{1}{2}$ sec from a medal.

'Bunny' Field was fourteen years old, and at school in Switzerland, when she was spotted as a likely Olympic prospect by Mrs. Ros Hepworth, a woman who does a tremendous amount of work for British skiing by organising training for junior skiers under the aegis of the Downhill Only Club in Wengen. Last year it looked as if all 'Bunny' Field's training would be wasted when she broke her ankle in Italy in August. On top of this she has also had a lot of problems with her health, which makes it even more amazing that she should have now smashed through into world class.

Both Nancy Greene and Divina Galica had better luck in the giant slalom race five days later. Over a course of nearly a mile Miss Greene skied with tremendous nerve and energy to take the gold medal by more than 2½ sec from the silver medalist, Annie Famose, of France. And Divina Galica, injured before the Games, shattered by her bad luck in the downhill event, had some compensation when she skied well enough to come eighth. So in the three women's events the British girls have come fourth in the slalom (Gina Hathorn), sixth in the downhill ('Bunny' Field), and eighth in the giant slalom. And that, for a lowland nation, is a truly fantastic result.

The British girls certainly provided a delightful diversion from the troubles of these commercial-ridden Games. Why the I.O.C. ever chose Grenoble to stage the Winter Games is beyond anyone's comprehension, for Grenoble is not a winter sports resort. As Avery Brundage himself remarked: 'These were not a Winter Olympics but a series of world championships.'

Only the skating events were held in Grenoble itself. The bobsleigh was at Alpe-d'Huez, the Alpine skiing in Chamrousse, the Nordic events in Autrans and the tobogganing events in Villard de Lans. To cover all the sites in one day involved over 250 miles of driving, most of it on mountain roads. It was as if Edinburgh had staged the Games and farmed out the Alpine skiing to Perth, the Nordic events to Stirling and the bobsleigh to some village over the English border. As a result it was only the skaters, and a few officials, who lived in the Olympic village in Grenoble— all the other competitors had to live at the sites of their various events. Hence the talk of these games being a series of disconnected world championships instead of an Olympic Games. But it was commercialism, and not the scattered nature of the Games, which produced the biggest row—and indeed nearly led to the cancellation of the Games.

Before the Games the President of the International Ski Federation, Mr. Marc Hodler of Switzerland, had promised Avery Brundage that all trade names and marks would be removed from competitors' skis. But when this decision was communicated to the council of the Federation they rejected it out of hand. And so did the skiers and team managers, who said that such a ban threatened the whole future of international skiing, which is heavily dependent on free equipment—and money— provided by the ski-makers.

This left Brundage in the humiliating position of announcing at a press conference that all makers' names would be removed and then being informed an hour later by Marc Hodler that they would not be! Eventually, on the very eve of the Games, a compromise was reached. The skiers would be allowed to keep names and trademarks on their skis but their skis would be taken away as soon as they had finished their race so that they could not be photographed with them.

It was an unsatisfactory compromise and one that led the I.O.C. to threaten ominously that 'The whole question of the Winter Olympic Games is being studied by a special committee of the I.O.C.'

But you cannot beat the ingenuity of manufacturers when they are bent on getting world-wide coverage for their goods. The very first event was the men's downhill race—the blue riband of the Games. Expecting trouble, I took up my position ten yards past the finishing line where I could get a good view of the officials rushing up to the competitors and taking their skis from them.

The favourite for the race was the twenty-four-year-old Frenchman Jean Claude Killy, a man who is regarded by the French people with a veneration that is, in British terms, a combination of our idolatry of W. G. Grace and Margot Fonteyn.

Killy's team-mate, Guy Perillat, had already set what seemed to be an unapproachable time with a descent of the most sublime beauty and technical skill. Perillat was the only one of the first thirteen runners to break two minutes for the course which was just short of two miles. His time: 1 min 59.93 sec, an average speed of nearly sixty miles an hour.

Now it was Killy, start number 14, who was waiting at the start with the knowledge that he did not have any wax on his skis. Earlier, while warming up, he hitched a ride on a small ski lift to take him back to the start and the icy track below the lift had scraped all the wax off his skis. Michel Arpin, Killy's technical advisor, was beside himself with worry: 'I thought it would be catastrophic.' Yet Killy was calm and I wonder how many other men in the world could have been calm in such circumstances, knowing that all France expected him to win. He held his goggles off his face to stop them steaming up, spat out his chewing gum, and then launched himself down the precipitous snow.

There was nothing pretty about his style—skis were often a

yard apart, arms flying, body rising to the vertical on the jumps instead of crouching in the streamlined egg position. But every movement spelt 'attack, attack, attack'. Twice he seemed to be out of control, yet he stuck savagely to his line, coming down from the air to bite his skis into a turn.

At the finish Perillat, the greatest skier in the world in 1961, an old man by Olympic standards, waited and waited, knowing that only Killy could deprive him of the gold medal. And Killy did so by eight hundredths of a second—an interval almost too brief for the human eye to detect. Killy too had raced down the course in under two minutes—his time was 1 min 59.85 sec against Perillat's 1 min 59.93 sec.

Before Perillat could walk across to Killy and congratulate him another skier with yellow bars across his black leather gloves and the word 'Dynamic' emblazoned across the pouch fastened to his back, rushed across to Killy and hugged him interminably. A few minutes later, when a policeman came to take Killy's skis away from him, the man with the yellow-barred gloves bent down, took off one of his own skis and stuck it into the snow. There, on the tip of the ski just alongside Killy's head, were two more yellow bars.

Fifty rioting French photographers recorded the moment while above them the colour television cameras sent the image of those yellow bars across Europe and across the United States of America.

Marc Hodler, the charming Swiss lawyer, President of the International Ski Federation, the man who had promised Avery Brundage that there would be no advertising of skis at the Olympic Games, tried to remove the man with the yellow-barred gloves, but the damage was done. Now the skiing world knew that Jean Claude Killy had flashed down the course reaching a maximum speed of eighty-seven miles per hour on 'Dynamic' skis to win the most coveted gold medal of the Winter Olympics.

It was the gloves that were the master stroke. They were worn by Killy's technical adviser Michel Arpin, one-time member of the French ski team and now a representative of the firm Dynamic which supplies skis to a large proportion of the downhill competitors, and which uses as its trade-mark two yellow bars.

French television showed that kiss of victory at least a dozen times in the next forty-eight hours and each time the yellow-barred gloves were prominently in the picture. What a simple way to thwart Mr. Avery Brundage and the International Olympic Committee, who, only three days before, had patiently debated for five and a half hours in an effort to produce that compromise and eliminate commercialism from these games.

Brundage did not see Killy's victory. He refused to attend the Alpine skiing events in protest at having to compromise over his decision not to allow trade-marks on skis. I sympathised with him and for the first time in my life I felt intense admiration for him. I could feel the pull of his idealism, even though it seems that the idealistic course which he is setting will end in the sea with Brundage standing on the beach like King Canute, bidding the tide to recede.

When Michel Arpin had finished his publicity kiss, Perillat, his sad face torn by a weak smile of congratulation, walked across to Killy and kissed him on both cheeks. All the hope, effort and tension of years of struggle for supreme mastery in one field of human endeavour was synthesised in that moment. And there was Arpin still flapping his yellow-barred gloves. Damn him and his sordid little stunt.

It was precisely what Brundage had feared: that the moment of victory, the moment when you win a lead-filled, gold-plated medal worth only a few shillings, the moment when you prove your complete mastery, would be sullied by materialism.

Brundage sees it as a bad example to the youth of the world for whom the Olympic movement exists. He sees purity sullied by modern materialism and he will fight to preserve the ideal which he and his venerable committee believe in.

Before I went to Grenoble I believed the Olympics, the supreme championships of the world, were strong enough to overcome all commercial pressures, but now I doubt it. Everywhere in Grenoble there was evidence of split thinking, of bewilderment of where to draw the line. For instance, while the I.O.C. and the International Ski Federation debated for many hours about trade-marks on skis, no one so much as mentioned that there was also advertising—the word 'Grenoble'—on the competitors' numbers. Indeed, Killy skied with the name 'Grenoble' on his chest and with the name of Val d'Isère, his home ski resort on his helmet.

What is the difference between advertising a resort and advertising a brand of equipment?

I asked this question of Marc Hodler and his reply was: 'Well, you see, the resorts lose money on staging these races so we allow them to use their names on the bibs.' What Mr. Hodler is saying is that the resorts could not afford to stage the skiing events unless they were allowed some advertising, but then no skier could possibly afford to compete in international competition today (unless he be the Aga Khan) if he is not given assistance from the ski manufacturers, who also, like the resorts, want to recoup their outlay through advertising.

The trouble is that skiing is becoming the victim of its own success. It is now one of the largest recreational sports in the world and therefore an industry has grown up behind it. It is the same in many other sports. Once the youth of the world starts to take part—the essence of the Olympic ideal—they need equipment and facilities. Industry supplies the equipment and does so with great generosity often beyond the dictates of pure commerce. And in return they want to be allowed to do a little advertising. Government, cities and resorts provide the facilities (it cost the city of Grenoble and France itself almost £100,000,000 to stage the Games) and they too want to recoup some of their outlay by advertising and thus getting tourists to visit their facilities.

So where do you draw the line? Do you restrict the Olympics so that only true amateurs can compete, thus contracting the games so that even the smallest town could stage them? Or do the I.O.C. try to ride the band-wagon? A line must be drawn somewhere.

It cannot be the amateur line, for the only true amateurs in sport these days are those who are no good at it. What would be the point of an Olympics that was restricted to the 'scrubber'— the tourist skier, the club athlete—and to those born of rich parents? Yet the Olympics cannot be allowed to be submerged in materialism, so there must be compromise, unsatisfactory and imperfect though that be.

I would like to suggest that the best sportsmen in the world should be allowed to compete whether they be amateur or professional but that it should be made abundantly clear that they will do so on neutralised equipment (already one class of yachtsman in the Summer Olympics have to draw their boats from a common pool). It should also be made abundantly clear that no advertising whatsoever, be it skis, or resorts, will be allowed for the entire period of the Games; and that all tricks like Michel Arpin's yellow-barred gloves will lead to instant disqualification. There is something in the Olympics, indefinable, springing from the soul, that must be preserved.

But let us get back to the action. It is impossible to chronicle everything that happens at an Olympic Games, even to chronicle everything that happens at the Winter Games, which, in comparison to the Summer Games, are still relatively small. But I must record briefly that Eugenio Monti of Italy, the Scobie Breasley of the bob-sledding world, at last achieved his final dream—an Olympic gold medal. World champion nine times, he had, until the morning of February 11th, failed to win an Olympic title. He did it by the narrowest of margins, for the aggregate time, over four runs, of his two-man bob was exactly tied by the German pair of Floth and Bader. For interminable minutes we waited thinking that Monti would only have the satisfaction of a divided gold medal, until at last the announcement came over the loudspeaker that the title would go to the team which had recorded the fastest single run. And that was Monti, bow-legged and scarred, the greatest driver of a two-man bob the world has ever seen.

I must record also that Peggy Flemming, a nineteen-year-old raven-haired American girl from Colorado Springs, won, as everyone expected her to, the figure-skating gold medal. She was technically superb and yet there was something strangely disappointing about her performance. Figure-skating is a sport which is sometimes lifted, by rare practitioners, into an art. Who can forget the skating of Donald Jackson, the Canadian who electrified the sport in the early 1960s with performances that were much more than just sport. But Miss Flemming is not that sort of skater. In the words of Dick Button, the American Olympic champion in 1948 and 1952, she tends to be a little dull. Perhaps a fairer word would be 'cool'—as cool as the lime-green dress she wore.

One pair of skaters did at least lift sport into the realms of art—the Protopopovs, Ludmila and Oleg, four times European champions, three times world champions, twice Olympic champions in the pairs skating.

There were those who prophesied that they were over the top, that Ludmila had had a bad fall in November and now had to skate with a bandaged knee. True, she did, but it didn't affect their performance. There were moments when your breath was sucked out of your body in sheer wonder at their beauty of movement and that, after all, is what they were trying to do. 'Art,' said Oleg, afterwards, 'cannot be measured by points. We skate from the heart. To us it is spiritual beauty that matters.'

As he talked, diplomatically and vivaciously, he held Ludmila's hand between his own. She is so delicate, like a piece of Meissen porcelain, and all the time she watches him talk with those large eyes set above the high Slav cheekbones.

Coming from such a man there is no hint of corn when he talks of their love. 'First of all I see in what we try to do, a man and a woman. These pairs of brother and sister, how can they convey the emotion—the love that exists between a man and a woman? That is what we try to show.'

There was one moment when they were as one person: she, like a swan in flight, tucked underneath him, dominated by him, until he let her go and she glided forward, a beautiful woman leaving her lover, showing the world her affection, her contentment.

In contrast there was the shabby incident of the three East German girls in the tobogganing events who heated the runners of their sleds just before the start to give them greater speed. This is entirely against the rules because it ruins the ice-covered run and they were promptly disqualified.

The Games ended, as they had begun, with yet another row. It was an unfortunate one and I still do not know the truth of the affair, but it was certainly a sad one for the great Austrian skier Karl Schranz and for Jean Claude Killy who was bidding, in the men's slalom on the final Saturday, for his third gold medal —a feat only accomplished once before—in 1956 by Toni Sailer.

The slalom was held in appalling conditions at Chamrousse. Visibility was down to ten or fifteen yards—a day when you ski with your eyeballs scraping the snow. The event is decided on the aggregate time of two courses. On the first course Killy was fastest with a time of 49.37 sec and Schranz was third fastest with 49.69 sec. The start of the second run had to be delayed because the visibility was getting even worse. Time after time Killy went into the starting gate only to be brought back when the visibility was reduced to under ten yards. But eventually, threequarters of an hour late, Killy burst out of the gate with his usual attacking style to record a time of 50.36 sec. Six start numbers later came Schranz. The television cameras glimpsed him through the mist, but then he disappeared—a sign that he had fallen. But it was not so. He had stopped at gate number 22, saying that he had missed gates number 18 and 19 because a soldier had skied across the course at gate number 22, thus distracting his attention.

Colonel Readhead, of Britain, the start referee, therefore allowed Schranz to start again and when he did he came down in 49.53 sec and the gold medal was his. So for an hour it seemed that the Austrian men, long the best skiers in the world, had at last won a gold medal in these Grenoble Games. But the chief of the race, a Monsieur Esnault of France, was not satisfied. He positioned himself at gate 22 and asked the late starters, the 'scrubbers', whether they could see him when they were going through gates 18 and 19. They reported that they could not. So the jury deliberated and decided that Schranz should be disqualified for missing gates 18 and 19 on that first abortive run of the second slalom.

The rule is that if a competitor is baulked during a run he is allowed to start again pending a full examination of the circumstances of his first run. So now Schranz loses his second run—his winning run—because of his disqualification on the first run. It is a little complicated, but, in effect, the jury are saying that Schranz's story of why he stopped at gate number 22 is not true. How many times in Olympic history has the apparent winner been accused of such a thing? I cannot remember any such incident ever happening before.

The rejection of Schranz's word must have been a shattering blow for him, for he has made his life in skiing. After this affair what sort of a reputation can he have? I also feel sorry for Killy because this man desperately wanted to win all three Alpine gold medals, but he, I am sure, wanted to win all three on the slopes and not in the committee rooms.

Killy has now no more honours to win in skiing. Where can he go from here? Nominally he has a job as a Customs officer in Val d'Isère, but this is purely a device to give him a regular pay packet and yet stay within the amateur rules. He could go to America and manage one of their booming ski resorts. He could stay in Val d'Isère and carry on the now well-established family business—his father is an hotelier and sports-shop owner. But will this ever be enough for him?

He must have a challenge and he has found it in other ways than in skiing: in bull-fighting, for instance, which he discovered in Nimes; or in motor racing at which he is superlatively good, having won the two-litre class in last year's Targo Florio, driving a Porsche.

But perhaps it is the quieter, more contemplative side of Killy that is a truer guide to his character and his future. His room in Val d'Isère is full of Savoy antiques and pleasant pictures—a restful, thoughtful room with no cups or trophies; the room of a man who, despite his untutored mind (he left school at fifteen), has tried to keep his brain free from rust.

One has the feeling that he would like the next challenge to be to his brain. But such is the way of the world that I doubt if anyone will lay down that challenge. At twenty-four, Jean Claude Killy's life has come to its climax—never again will he experience such fulfilment. Of course, he will go on trying, seeking for a perfection of life that will satisfy his mind as well as his body—the quest of a rare champion, a great champion.

3
'ONLY THE BRITISH WOULD BE GENTLEMEN'

Lake Tahoe is an emerald lake, glittering and clear, twenty-two miles long by twelve miles wide, set in a bowl of mountains. To those early American pioneers trekking westward to the promised land, parched by the Nevada desert, racked by the long haul up yet another mountain range, it must have seemed like the Promised Land, the jewel in the forehead of America.

Tahoe, which means 'the lake set in the skies', might have remained unspoilt if it hadn't been for the strange accident of the American gambling laws. It lies on the state border between California (which does not allow gambling) and Nevada (which does allow gambling). So, right on the state line, on the south shore of Lake Tahoe, the gambling casinos have risen above the pine trees. They lie like a raw slash across the throat of the beautiful lake—ten miles of neon signs and clapboard motels.

Fourteen thousand people live on the south shore of Lake Tahoe and they have begun to realise that the tourism and gambling by which they live are ruining one of the most beautiful spots in the world. Imbued with a new community spirit, they looked around to see what they could do to help the community—and help themselves with a little favourable publicity. So they worked out a scheme to provide a summer home for the American Olympic team—a high-altitude home. Lake Tahoe itself is at 6000 feet and the roads that lead out of the basin climb to a height of 7400 feet, the same height as Mexico City. So the community of South Lake Tahoe spent £125,000 on making sure that 'our Olympic boys have the best'. Intrigued by reports of great happenings in this American paradise in the skies—a new world record of 44.0 sec for the 400 metres and a new world record of 19.7 sec for the 200 metres—I flew to Tahoe *en route* to Mexico City.

There I found that we poor, gentlemanly British had been taken for mugs. You will remember the rule about altitude training passed by the International Olympic Committee, the rule which says: 'That to achieve fairness as far as possible between competitors, no athlete, other than those who usually live and train at such heights, shall specially do so at high altitudes for more than four weeks in the last three months before the opening of the Games.'

The British Olympic team have religiously abided by this rule. The American track team have not. The majority of their athletes set up camp at Echo Summit (which lies at a height of 7400 feet) in the middle of July and have been training there on a specially constructed tartan track. Some of their officials say, cynically, that they took attorney's advice on the I.O.C. rule. Apparently this attorney's advice was that the four weeks specified in the rule only applied when the athletes were together as the official Olympic team.

So the ruse they adopted was that all training from July 15th to the middle of September, when their final Olympic trials ended, was termed 'The South Lake Tahoe United States Olympic Medical and Testing Programme'. But the rule does not use the word 'team', so it is hard to see any justification beyond that given to me by one of the officials: 'Hell, what do you expect us to do—give the Russkies the gold medals on a plate? They have been at Alma Ata for months, maybe years.'

That is probably true. In fact, if rumour is to be believed, it would be difficult to find any of the major teams, except for the British and Australians, who have honoured the rules. The American athletes report, for instance, that the West German team have been in Flagstaff, Arizona, at 7000 feet for a month.

It was, I suppose, all very predictable. When the rule was published after the I.O.C.'s session in Rome in April 1966 we pointed out that it would be an impossible rule to enforce and said that 'only the British would be gentlemen'. But, of course, the Olympics these days are not for gentlemen, for there is too much national prestige at stake. Yet I am surprised that the Americans have flaunted the rules so brazenly, especially when one remembers that an American, Avery Brundage, is the President of the I.O.C. And especially when one remembers that second, idealistic paragraph of the rule which states: 'The I.O.C. points out that to break this rule would be a gross breach of good sportsmanship, and it is sure that no one connected with the Olympic movement would wish in any way to be guilty of taking an unfair advantage over the other competitors.'

Wondering whether Avery Brundage knew that the American track and field team had been breaking this rule, I telephoned him in his office in the plush La Salle Hotel in Chicago. The sprightly eighty-one-year-old President of the I.O.C. is not given to expressions of amazement—if he was he would have been in a perpetual state of amazement over this year's Olympic happenings—but there was no doubt the news was a surprise, and a shock, to him.

'That's not very good—and right here in the United States,' he said. 'That's pretty serious. I'll have to try to reach the U.S. Olympic Committee, if I can find them.'

I gave Brundage twenty-four hours to get to work and then telephoned the two men principally involved—Hilmer Lodge, Chairman of the United States Olympic Track and Field Committee, and Douglas Robey, the President of the whole U.S. Olympic Committee. Hilmer Lodge did not try to deny the fact that many members of the American track and field team had been at Echo Summit for far longer than the statutory four weeks. He said that he and his committee felt that they owed it to their boys to give them an opportunity of long-term training at high altitude—'as so many other countries are doing'. I respected him for his openness, but I certainly did not respect the attitude of Douglas Robey. When he discovered that it was I who had phoned Avery Brundage he shouted down the telephone: 'What do you think you are—a detective? We have not broken the rules. I am not going to talk to you.' And then he slammed down the telephone.

To me the most annoying part of the whole affair is that I now fear for the chances of Dave Hemery, the British 400 metres hurdler, who has, in my opinion, an outstanding chance of winning a gold medal. But his two chief rivals, Ron Whitney and

Geoff Vanderstock, have both been up here training for well over the statutory four weeks.

Now the 400 metres hurdles is not an event in which altitude is vital, but some of the American athletes here tell me that those people who have been at altitude for a long period have a considerable advantage when the competition takes place under Olympic conditions, i.e. heats on the first day, semi-finals on the second day, and then the final on the third day. Apparently those who are well acclimatised are able to throw off the fatigue of the heats and semi-finals, whereas those who have only had a short time at altitude find that they have got no fire left in their bodies by the time they reach the final.

To be fair to the American athletes themselves, I don't think that they had known of the rule. They just came here, to Lake Tahoe, to get in shape for the Games, and a magnificent job they have done of it.

Their camp consists of a row of large caravans parked in the forest behind a highway maintenance depot at the top of a pass which leads from Lake Tahoe to the Californian state capital of Sacramento. Just across the road, the citizens of South Lake Tahoe have built the athletes a brand-new tartan track surrounded by huge ponderosa pines.

The athletes work desperately hard on this pleasant track. They are tuned to perfection and honed by the most fearsome selection process imaginable. The American selectors took the easy way out. After dithering about various selection methods they went back, at the last moment, to the time-honoured system of saying it would be a do-or-die trials. The first three in every event, regardless of accident, regardless of the season's form, would be selected.

'You can't imagine what it was like up here,' one of them told me. 'There were ten of us for every event. We had trained together, lived together, become friends. Then on the appointed day the gun was loaded and seven were shot down. The strain was just too much for some of them. Dave Patrick (the American 1500 metres champion this year) sat and watched the events day by day—it went on for ten days, scheduled exactly like the Olympic programme—and saw these great athletes getting shot down.

'Bob Schul and Billy Mills, both Olympic champions—out. Men who had high-jumped 7 ft 2 in. or run 200 metres in 20.1 sec—out. Not even allowed to stay and watch the rest of the trials. They were given just twenty-four hours to pack their bags and get the hell out of here.

'When it came to the 1500 metres final on the last day, Patrick, who had the best time in the semi-finals, was shot to hell—nerves jangling raw. He came down that finishing straight and when he was twenty yards from the tape he realised he couldn't make it, and he started to pummel his knees with his fists. Yes, men just went away into the woods and wept. Years of work, the best shape they'd ever been in in their lives, performances that would have got them into any other nation's team, and all they got was twenty-four hours to pack their bags. Mexico will be a cake-walk in comparison.'

It is not surprising that the survivors are now favourites to take fifteen of the twenty-four gold medals at stake in the men's track and field programme at the Games.

Of course, I inquired about the threatened boycott of the team by some of the Negro athletes which would seriously reduce America's chances of gold medals in the short-distance events. One of the athletes told me that the boycott was now a dead issue. 'You remember Bob Hayes (the 100 metres gold medallist in Tokyo)?' he said. 'You remember the big fat contract he got afterwards to become a professional footballer? Well, some of the big professional football teams started to ring up one or two of our sprint stars and talk turkey about contracts after Mexico, but they always made one proviso: "We don't want no racial trouble. Cut out this boycott talk." Man, the boycott doesn't stand a chance against the hard fact that a gold medal is a meal ticket for life for some of them.'

But it is not all as cynical as that. When you forget the cynicism of some of the officials, and the nationalistic drum-beating, there is, among the athletes themselves, a tremendous Olympic spirit, and I am sure they are going to live up to their advanced billing in Mexico City. I only hope that this long period of acclimatisation at high altitude does not give Whitney and Vanderstock too much of an advantage over Dave Hemery, who is the most likely British athlete to win a gold medal in Mexico.

4
'WE ARE FIGHTING FOR MEXICO'

They were killing people when I arrived in Mexico City on the night of Wednesday, October 2nd.

It is one of the strange phenomena of Mexico City that a battle can be taking place in one part of the city, while the plush 'Pink Zone' of the city dances and drinks the night away. I drove from the airport into the centre of the city, picked up a hired car, and drove out to the press centre at the Olympic village, and I still didn't know that anything was going on.

At midnight, three hours after landing in Mexico, I was leaning over a desk in the press centre, having what was to prove the first of an interminable number of arguments about accommodation, when two Australian journalists walked into the building and said that at least twenty-five people had been killed in a square, one mile north of the city centre.

This book is a diary of the Games and you may think that the battle that took place that night has nothing to do with the Olympics. If so, then I would advise you to skip this chapter. But I believe that you cannot divorce sport from the environment in which it is held. That battle had much to do with the Games. For the first time for many years journalists from all over the world descended on Mexico and they were free to report to the world what they saw. This was an opportunity that the deep-rooted protest movement could not ignore. Their own press is very much an 'Establishment' press—another arm of the ruling P.R.I. (Partido Revolucionario Institucionalista)—the party which has ruled Mexico since 1928. So it is no coincidence that the battle took place at a time when the eyes of the world were turned towards Mexico and the world could see that it was not the stable and progressive regime that it is always made out to be.

To me, one of the minor attractions of a sporting journalist's life is that I am able to visit many different countries in the world and, through the universal camaraderie of sport, get to know something about their philosophy and way of life.

To land in the middle of a battle is a stark way of doing this. It was fascinating, and horrifying. I believe that an account of what happened and how it happened is very necessary to an understanding of Mexico and its peoples. The Olympics was, after all, their showpiece—their party face. Behind that face there is another stark, tumultuous face—a face that has little regard for the sanctity of human life.

Before you read on, just imagine the furore in Britain if even two or three people were killed in a civil disorder. Well, that night in Mexico City dozens of people, of all ages, died; and even now, a month after the battle, nobody knows their number. The official figure is thirty-four, but nobody believes this. Some people estimate that as many as 200, maybe even 500, people died that night. My own estimate, based on countless discussions, is that the number is probably about eighty. Why did it happen? Let a schoolteacher, whom I met with my colleague, Hugh McIlvanney, in the Plaza of the Three Cultures the next day, speak for them:

'We are not interested in being with Mao, with Castro, with the Vatican, with Johnson, with the left or with the right. We are not interested in labels. We are fighting for Mexico, for our liberty, for our constitution. We want better homes, better food, better health for our children. All this we can have if our constitution is respected. That is all we ask.'

But the night before they had had a very specific demand to make. Five thousand people, the majority of them students, gathered in the Plaza of the Three Cultures. Their object was to call upon the army to withdraw from the Polytechnic buildings, which had been occupied since the students' riots in September.

The Plaza has been a natural choice for large public meetings in Mexico City since the protest movement acquired momentum after the first serious clash with the authorities on July 26th. It is a huge square, bounded on one side by a preparatory school of the Polytechnic, while on another side there is a vast block of workers' flats with balconies that make convenient platforms for the speakers. Many of the tenants of the flats have given support to the students, and harboured those harassed by the security forces. The balconies look out across a paved area of almost two acres, over the ruins of an Aztec pyramid and an ancient ball court, to a main road. In the centre a magnificent Colonial church is dwarfed by the matchbox tower of the Ministry of Foreign Affairs. The blend of Aztec, Colonial and severely modern architecture gives the Plaza its name.

When the meeting started the first speaker announced a change of plan. 'The meeting will finish here. Afterwards everyone must go home. We know that the army is going to provoke us if we march in procession to Santo Thomaso.'

A colleague, John Rodda of the *Guardian*, was on another balcony close to the speaker. What happened to him is baffling but significant. From behind the church, over this peaceful meeting, two green Very lights arched into the air. Sensing trouble, he turned to find a pistol being pointed at him by a man in civilian clothes. He was ordered harshly to lie down. Within seconds the Plaza was a battleground. Two helicopters cruised overhead and some people alleged that machine-guns were fired from their open doors.

The next two hours were the most horrifying of the whole of Rodda's life. He lay on the balcony while bullets whistled overhead, and the square in front of him was turned into a battlefield. But the most significant thing, in our quest to find out who was guilty of this outrage, is that eventually Rodda was able to establish that the men behind the pistols—the men who were there just before the shooting started—were security police. Each wore one white glove to identify him to the others.

Rodda himself has no proof of how many died in the square that night, but one reporter from United Press International, the American agency, himself counted twenty-five dead, and one man cannot cover such a big area. Two hours later, in the middle of the night, special buses arrived outside one of the Olympic press centres, and hurried reporters to the Presidential Palace. The President's Press Secretary announced twenty dead and seventy-five 'slightly wounded'. Apparently there were no seriously wounded. In answer to a question he remarked with a smile that he could not time the duration of the battle as a sportswriter might have done.

Next morning, as rumours swept the press centre that sniping was still going on, Princess Grace of Monaco, in a cool white hat, smiled and nodded her way past the Telex machines clattering out the story of the carnage. In the plush Camino Real, Mexico City's newest hotel (the deep red carpets on the staircases lead up to golden walls, a log fire burns before empty leather sofas—each ten feet wide—and there is space and tranquillity and opulence), the I.O.C. Executive Committee met in emergency session to decide whether the Games should go on. Eventually, Avery Brundage issued a statement: 'The Games of the 19th Olympiad, a friendly gathering of the youth of the world, in amicable competition, will proceed as scheduled. . . . As guests of Mexico, we have full confidence that the Mexican people, universally known for their great sportsmanship and great hospitality, will join the participants and spectators in celebrating the Games, a veritable oasis in a troubled world.'

At the Plaza of the Three Cultures the soldiers slept on the steps or queued for tortillas and beans. There had been rumours of sniping, but in fact there had only been one untraced shot. Who could start anything in broad daylight when faced with upwards of 3000 soldiers, scores of armoured cars and dozens of jeeps, each with a machine-gun mounted on the platform?

On the streets the newspaper headlines alleged foreign interference; accused extremists and Castro-ites. In our hotel room that night a university lecturer, an anthropology student, a civil servant and his wife talked calmly: 'You must realise that we have had the same political party in power since 1928, and, of the succession of Presidents produced by this party, our present President, Gustavo Diaz Ordaz, is the worst. He is inefficient, yet he has taken power completely into his hands. He is not interested in money for himself, but he has made sure that his family have wealth. One of his sons was given a contract for the underground system. He does not do the work. He sub-contracts but the money comes through his hands.'

Despite this indictment, the original aim of the protest movement—an alliance of students, the progressive middle class, and workers resentful of union subordination to the regime—was not the removal of President Diaz Ordaz. They simply wanted a return to the constitution ('we have one of the most advanced constitutions in the world, but Diaz Ordaz has stamped on it') and the end of repression. But now, sickened by the killings of these last three months, the movement has changed its objectives. Its members are beginning to feel that President Diaz Ordaz is discredited beyond redemption.

Perfectly ordinary middle-class people who would not have looked out of place at an English church social described to us in detail the government's technique for wiping out all traces of some of those who had died in the riots. They talked of bodies being burned, documents being confiscated and destroyed, of names being eradicated from official registers and families terrorised into silence.

There are few countries in which such stories would be given credence. But in Mexico, where nine million of the forty million people cannot read or write, where government officials speak of 'only' twenty-five dead, where an eight-year-old girl selling us a newspaper at one o'clock in the morning stands aside to let a beautiful young woman in arctic fox step into a Cadillac—anything seems possible.

A student told us: 'The world should know that the economic and political stability of Mexico is a myth.' But why did that instability cost so many lives in the Plaza of the Three Cultures?

Some diplomatic observers believe that the students went prepared for a bloody fight; that they installed five machine-guns in empty flats; that the shooting of a paratroop general early in the battle showed that there was nothing haphazard about their fire; that 200 security police infiltrated the meeting intent on arresting the student leaders.

Some Mexicans say, on the contrary, that this is not a simple conflict between students and government. There is, they believe, a third force at work: the army. They point out that there are certain soldiers—not necessarily at the top—who would like to see Diaz Ordaz so discredited that they could seize control of the country. They are convinced that it was the army that provoked Wednesday night's showdown. They say that the Very lights were a signal for a planned slaughter. They say that soldiers in civilian clothes fired from amongst the students to justify the massive retaliation. They say that agents from the government, the army and the police were shooting from the flats and on the roof-tops, escalating the incident into a battle. They concede that some of the tenants and some students had arms and were using them: 'But if the students had been as well armed as we are told, if they had had machine-guns, would only two soldiers have been killed and nineteen wounded?'

Certainly the theory of a deliberately engineered clash makes sense of John Rodda's account of the massacre. Nearly every Mexican we have met believes that it was the army that provoked this showdown. A typical reaction is: 'We think the students are trying to do something right and clean because they want to do it in front of the people. They have asked for a public dialogue on the restoration of constitutional rights. They want an enquiry into the responsibility for the shooting, one that must be held in front of the Press, television and the ordinary people.'

Far from getting such an enquiry, they have been driven underground. Seventy out of 180 members of the movement's National Strike Committee have been arrested. Two are dead. Those detained are said to be undergoing torture. But new members have been elected to take their places. They flit from hideout to hideout, meeting secretly, never in the same place twice.

Members of the committee say that they do not want to stop the Olympic Games. But they feel the money spent on the Games should have been used to attack the grotesque anomalies of the Mexican society.

'If the government are so smart that they can persuade the world to let them hold the Olympic Games they should be able to solve the problems at home.'

There is considerable uneasiness about the Olympics, which are now only ten days away. One member of the I.O.C. told me: 'We have a terrible responsibility. It only needs someone to throw a squib at the opening ceremony to start a panic.' But certainly the I.O.C. Executive Committee are refusing to be rushed into hasty statements.

And this is probably very wise. What we need now, above all, is a period of calm, a period in which life can get back to normal—if the pre-Olympic period can ever be considered normal.

5
'FEAR IS THE GREATEST SPUR'

Friday, October 11th

Tomorrow, at last, the wholesomeness at the heart of this frenzied affair will break through and overwhelm the neurosis of the past week. Or so we fervently hope. Tomorrow the Games will open and then, finally, on Sunday, we shall get the first action.

At five o'clock on Sunday afternoon, give or take *uno momentito* or two (and that can be anything from fifteen minutes to two hours), fifty-two men will line up for the start of 'murder'.

Thankfully, the murder has nothing to do with last week's carnage in the Plaza of the Three Cultures, and, hopefully, nothing like that will happen again until after the Games are over, for there is an uneasy truce in Mexico City.

The 'murder' refers simply to twenty-five laps of the Olympic track by fifty-two of the world's best athletes who step out tomorrow to run the 10,000 metres. The words come, in a thick Irish accent, from Jim Hogan, the Chiswick groundsman, marathon champion of Europe, a man who is realistic enough to know that he will not win.

It seems strange to be talking of sport here in a country where ten million people are hungry and where others are prepared to die in the cause of social justice. But life is lived on many levels, and the simplest, most basic level is the struggle of man against man. This struggle is at the heart of the frenzy that has gripped Mexico City this past week.

Men sit for days in a seventh-floor office of a glass-and-concrete building on the wide tree-lined Avenue Reforma—the headquarters of the organising committee—and plead, cajole and fly into tantrums in vain attempts to get themselves accredited to the Games. And the Mexicans, wishing to please everybody, wishing to show the world that they do not still sleep under a sombrero, tie themselves into bureaucratic knots piling two into a bed in the Olympic village press centre—now known as Stalag Luft Prensa.

It is hard to keep one's judgment, still harder to keep one's temper. One sees every facet of man's character—and some of it is sickening.

There are, for instance, two brothers here—Horst Dassler and Armin Dassler: they both run sports shoe firms—making at least 6000 pairs a day. And they cannot sell that quantity unless every schoolboy, every Sunday footballer, every businessman exercising in his health club, wants to wear the same shoes that this or that Olympic champion wore. So they bribe these amateur athletes—$7000 to one athlete, the nearest certainty to a gold medal in the Olympic village, is the highest price that I know.

Another athlete, also a potential gold medallist, accepted $1000 from Herr Horst Dassler's firm—known as Adidas—and then some time later said that it was not enough. He was given another $1500. Some time later he was approached by Herr Armin Dassler's firm—Puma—and signed an agreement to wear their shoes in exchange for $4000. Now, having banked $6500, he goes back to Adidas and asks for another $2500 'to complete my education'.

Whom do you blame—the athletes or the men who offer the money? Perhaps the root of this shoddy bargain lies in our own nature in that we are prepared to pay £2 more to have some vicarious contact with a champion rather than buy an equally good football boot or training shoe whose symbol has never been implanted in our minds.

Of course, it makes one wonder whether the whole Games have not reached such unruly proportions that all that was good in their original conception has been lost.

My faith, shattered into despair, was fleetingly restored yesterday by some unbelievable children's paintings. They stand, each 8 ft by 6 ft, tied to the railings of Chapultepec Park through which you pass *en route* to the stadium where the gymnasts will weave their heart-stopping patterns.

These paintings have the simplicity of the children who made them. There is expressed in them such clichés as the brotherhood of man and man's endeavour which reaches beyond the bounds of possibility, beyond all reason. But this, surely, is the simple truth and if this is what the Olympics mean to the children of the world then all the frenzy is worth while.

Never has there been so much frenzy—never have the Olympics so engaged the world's attention, never has there been such argument, such trauma. Yet I believe it will all die down tomorrow when man is pitted against man, woman against woman. (And of the last fact we can be sure, for they have all passed the sex test!)

Tomorrow we shall all know what altitude does to a man who has steeled himself to run for the supreme prize. We have talked and written and theorised, but not one of us really knows—for no amount of research, no amount of competition, can reproduce the conditions of an Olympic final.

By some fortuitous act of theatre the first final of the Games will be the 10,000 metres—the event in which altitude will play a major role. There are men who think that its role is so predominant that nobody who normally lives and competes at sea-level will stand a chance.

That is what Ron Clarke has been saying, but his words are only another 'con job' in a village where nearly 8000 athletes are trying to con each other in the world's largest gamesmanship centre. Clarke is a frightened man, and that is just as it should be. 'Fear is the greatest spur,' he says, 'no doubt about it.'

He is 'the greatest athlete the world has ever seen'. The words are those of Gabriel Karobkov, the chief Russian coach, and they are repeated by Franz Stampfl, the Viennese boulevardier, the man behind Bannister's victories in 1954, the man whom Clarke waited for before making up his mind on the tactics to adopt.

Clarke is the world-record holder, a man who has brought new standards to the sport, who has towed many lesser athletes to national records, a man who, at sea-level, would be an odds-on favourite. He is respected, acknowledged to be the greatest, by every distance runner in the world, yet his image is that of the loser. It is an image based on two races—the 10,000 metres in the 1964 Olympics at Tokyo and the 10,000 metres in the 1966 Commonwealth Games at Kingston, Jamaica.

In the first he won a bronze medal, in the second a silver medal. So he is the man who can shatter world records with a metronome rhythm but cannot win the big race.

Tomorrow is his last chance. Nobody knows this better than himself, for he is already thirty-one years old. 'All I know,' he says, with pain in his face like a man under torture, 'is that if I bloody miss this . . .' He cannot complete the sentence.

The betting is that he *will* miss it. The feeling amongst the athletes is that some unknown who lives and trains at altitude will shatter far greater athletes just because his heart and lungs and blood are adapted to withstand oxygen starvation.

Clarke has said so himself, but he will confess—provided the information is not published before Sunday—that he has only done so in order to put the pressure on himself and make the others 'believe that I have given the race away. I know that it sounds as if I have been making excuses for myself, but that is the only way I can make them lead.'

This is what he will do: for the first half of the race he will lie back, not bothering if someone makes a break, and keeping comfortably in the first third of the field. If someone breaks after half-distance he will go with them. If not, he will work his way through the field until he is poised with four laps to go. Then he will start to run—not with a sudden burst but with a steady increase of pace. They will keep with him, but he will keep going, relentlessly, until their legs turn to jelly. And then he will hang on, driven by fear, spurred by the thought that he, the greatest athlete in the world, will disgrace himself if he falters.

Bannister, in his description of the first four-minute mile, talked of falling into the arms of the world. Clarke, in his soul, is very like Bannister—too intelligent, too inhibited by thought, to run with the simple freedom that enables a man to break through the barriers of reason. That is what he has to do tomorrow if he is ever to be content with himself.

That is what it is all about—the fulfilment of oneself.

Of course, the world will see it differently: each nation revelling chauvinistically in the victories of its own athletes and mourning when their hopes are dashed.

But that is not the way it was ever meant to be or the way it is for any one of those 8000 athletes in the Olympic village this morning. They, in all their shapes and sizes, their colours and their creeds, have only one thing in common—the desire to excel for a few fleeting seconds or minutes before they return to their ordinary lives. That is what we have come here to see.

6
THE OPENING

Saturday, October 12th

Safely, with pomp and colour and with tears of relief, the 19th Olympiad of the Modern Era was declared open today by President Diaz Ordaz of Mexico. Nobody took a pot-shot at him.

It would have been very difficult for anyone to do so with 17,000 police, security men and soldiers ready to swivel on any untoward movement. What a relief it is. Now, at last, while an uneasy truce reigns between the Mexican Government and the protest movement, the Olympics can begin.

It was very like a grand family reunion—nearly 8000 athletes from more than 100 countries gathered together at last in this huge stadium. But it was some of the old familiar figures who caught my eye. There was Fanny Blankers-Koen, heroine of Wembley in 1948, now, at fifty years of age, thickening a little but still with a pair of legs that deserve a micro-mini skirt. There was Abebe Bikila carrying the Ethiopian flag, the man whose feet whispered in the dark over the Via Appia in Rome to take the marathon crown for the first time—a crown which, come tomorrow week, may still be his for the third Olympics.

There was Kiki Caron, the French swimmer, carrying her nation's flag and stopping the heart of every male in the stadium. She has one of those faces, proud with high cheekbones, that will last for ever. And there was the massive Zhabotinsky, twenty-seven stone of Russian man, world champion weight-lifter, the strongest man in the world, repeating the traditional Russian feat of marching the full circle of the arena with the flag held, one-handed, at arm's length.

But there was a new favourite today—a massive Mongolian

wrestler with bulging brown calf-length boots, bulging hairless thighs, a red bikini slip, and a huge expanse of bare chest. From his bare shoulders fluttered a pink, transparent cloak, a most feminine garment, yet carried with the bearing of Genghis Khan.

Of the teams, it was the Germans who first hit the eye—the West German girls in bitter orange being edged out of the fashion stakes by the East German girls in canary yellow. The prize for the nicest thought went to the Bulgars, tough-looking little men who fluttered posies of flowers before casting them into the crowd. But of course, it was the Czechs who stirred the crowd most.

Lynn Davies, the long-jumper, gold medal winner four years ago in Tokyo, carried the British flag and was embarrassed at the thought of having to march, an activity which appalls him as much as ballroom dancing. But, then, marching is foreign to all fit athletes who prize relaxation and suppleness of muscle. Lynn need not have worried. The medal for complete marching ineptitude went to the familiar figure (he appears at every Olympics) of the Afghan team manager who plonks one foot in front of the other in a loose imitation of the goosestep. And when the crowd cheers he accepts his medal with a wide grin and a boxer's handshake.

The British did not look good: white trousers, blue blazers and red polo-necked sweaters are a cluttering combination in a ceremony in which simplicity tells—like the simplicity of Enriqueta Basilio, the first woman to light the Olympic flame. The official handout says: 'She is tall, lean, with long legs and generally harmonious figure. Dark complexion, black hair and generally agreeable features.' She is all of that. A farm girl, twenty years old, from Baja California, she carried the torch gracefully around the track, and then, without faltering, bounced up ninety steps, the full height of the stadium, before turning and saluting the crowd with the symbolic flame.

It was all very familiar, exactly to the pattern laid down from Olympiad to Olympiad. Yet it was fresh and light-hearted; a perfect ceremony to set the tone for the next two weeks during which success will dominate the headlines, overshadowing the failure and disasters which make up so much of our normal daily reading diet.

As I write, streams of Mexicans file through the press seats eager to know how they did, what the world thinks of their five years of hard work. They have done well today and they have built some magnificent arenas for these games. If only the organisation and the transport were not so interminably slow!

Now the Games are properly launched—without any gun-fire, without an incident of any sort on this, the 476th anniversary of the discovery of the New World by Christopher Columbus.

7
'IN FAIR AND EQUAL COMPETITION'

Sunday, October 13th

Brian Corrigan is a doctor, a friend of Ron Clarke's. Just after five-thirty this afternoon he knelt on the grass of the Olympic Stadium, cradled Ron's head in his arms and wept. Clarke himself was unconscious, an oxygen mask clamped over his nose and mouth. They call this sport.

I feel bitter and angry. Altitude has now been proved to be the decisive factor. Altitude has turned one of the great races of the Olympic Games into a handicap event. The Olympic Charter talks about assembling the amateurs of all nations 'in fair and equal competition'. There is nothing fair or equal about these Games.

I am angry because I can hear 'knockers' at work already—the men who are saying that Ron Clarke cannot win the big event. He never stood a chance. He gave his heart today, he dredged the last ounce of his courage from his soul, and yet it was still not enough. Even in defeat this was Ron Clarke's day. This was the day on which he won the love and sympathy of all those who care for this great sport.

Thirty-seven men lined up for the start of the 10,000 metres—the only final to be held today. There were, amongst their number, seven men who were born and brought up in the highlands. There were also two, perhaps three, men who have spent a considerable part of the last two years training at altitude. And there was the remainder, twenty-seven or twenty-eight men, the finest distance runners in the world, who live and train at sea-level, and they were going to try to run this long, punishing race in an oxygen-starved atmosphere.

The early pace is slow, wisely slow for the sea-level men. Janos Szerenyi, a thirty-year-old Hungarian, a competent but not great performer, leads them through the first kilometre in 2 min 58.5 sec. Then Nickolay Sviridov, of Russia, takes the lead in the fifth lap and passes the 2000 metres mark in 5 min 57.4 sec. Compare this time with Ron Clarke's own world record in which he averaged 2 min 46 sec for each kilometre, which gives us a time of 5 min 32 sec for the 2000 metres. Already this field, the Olympic field, is running at a pace that is more than twenty-five seconds slower than Clarke's world record. Are these the Olympic Games?

Sviridov keeps the pace going very evenly at just under three minutes for every kilometre—8 min 56.1 sec for 3000 metres, 11 min 54.8 sec for 4000 metres. By now Clarke, who started very gently at the back of the field, has made his way up until he is in the first third. But at this pace everyone is bunched together and there is no sign of what is to come.

Then an Ethiopian, Wahib Masresha, takes over the work from Sviridov and passes the 5000 metres in 14 min 55 secs—more than a minute slower than Clarke's world record, and also approximately a minute slower than Clarke's run at the Crystal Palace last month. Another lap and the stadium almost explodes—Juan Martinez, in the red colours of Mexico, has gone into the lead and the vast Mexican crowd is beside itself with delight.

They cheer themselves almost into delirium for two and a half kilometres until Naftali Temu, small and slight and very black, and Ron Clarke, tall and swarthy and relaxed, take over the pacemaking. Then, suddenly, the small contingent of British spectators are electrified by the sight of Ron Hill, in bare feet and cut-away string vest, streaking into the lead. It's magnificent, but is it wise? Dr. Hill, a research chemist who lives in Cheshire, has only had three weeks' acclimatisation because he does not like to be separated from his family for too long. Surely his best tactics are to hang back and then use his finishing speed.

With four laps to go the race really begins. Mamo Wolde, the Ethiopian who came fourth in the 10,000 metres in Tokyo, hots up the pace and now only six other men can keep with him—Clarke, Temu, Gammoudi, Keino, Martinez and Sviridov. Of these, only Clarke can be said to have been anywhere near abiding by the Olympic rule of not spending more than four weeks training at altitude in the last three months before the Games, and even he has had just over five weeks. Of the remainder, Wolde, Temu, Keino and Martinez live at altitude, while both Gammoudi and Sviridov have spent months training in the hills. Ron Hill, a true amateur, who has abided by the rule, is some twenty yards back from the bunch.

As they came up to the finishing line, twenty-two laps behind them, three laps still to go, I expected Clarke to make his move. This would be the place, at sea-level, at which he should start to pulverise them with laps of sixty-four seconds. But that fabulous strength and rhythm of his is missing, and Wolde continues in the lead. With just over two and a half laps to go—sensation. Kipchoge Keino, one of the favourites, steps off the track and collapses on the grass. Now there are only four men in the race—Wolde, Temu, Clarke and Gammoudi.

With two laps to go Temu and Wolde accelerate and Clarke is dropped and then Gammoudi. At the bell Wolde is just in front of Temu with Gammoudi five yards back and Clarke well beaten. Round the top bend Wolde accelerates and flies down the back straight with Temu hanging on grimly two yards behind and beginning to look as if he is beaten. But even this wiry Ethiopian has no sprint left and, as they come into the finishing straight, Temu closes up to him and flashes by, finishing like a 1500 metres runner.

So Naftali Temu, a twenty-three-year-old private in the Kenyan Army, wins an Olympic gold medal to add to the gold medal which he won at the Commonwealth Games in Kingston, Jamaica. His time is 29 min 27.4 sec—108 sec slower than Clarke's world record and over ten seconds slower than Emil Zatopek's winning time in Helsinki in 1952, an age away in athletic terms.

Wolde is second, some four yards back, Gammoudi third in 29 min 34.2 sec, just in front of Juan Martinez of Mexico. Fifth is the Russian Sviridov, sixth an exhausted Ron Clarke and seventh a very gallant Ron Hill. And I should also record that Masresha of Ethiopia is eighth and Mejia of Columbia is tenth. So five of the first ten places are filled by men born and brought up in the highlands and there were only seven of them in the whole field.

Perhaps the most significant fact is that the Mexican Martinez could only finish ninth in this year's British championships, a purely domestic race, whereas here he can finish fourth against the finest runners in the world. Have we really seen 'fair and equal competition' today?

Let me not be unjust to Temu and Wolde. They are both brilliant runners. They may, indeed, have come first and second if the race had been run at sea-level. But we shall never know. We shall never know whether Temu is a worthy Olympic champion.

He started his career with two undistinguished performances in the 1964 Games—he dropped out of the 10,000 metres with two laps to go and he was 49th in the marathon. But we know he is a great runner, for did he not beat Clarke in the cauldron of Kingston, winning the Commonwealth Games gold medal. Yet Clarke has beaten him decisively this year—at sea-level.

Mamo Wolde, too, started his Olympic career with some undistinguished performances in 1956 in Melbourne when he was last in his heats of the 800 metres and 1500 metres. But in 1964 in Tokyo he was one of those who had the courage to hold on to Ron Clarke's pace in the 10,000 metres and finished in fourth position in a time that was fifty-six seconds faster than his time today. He is thirty-five years old, married with two children, and a corporal in the Imperial bodyguard. He is just under 5 ft 8 in. tall and weighs no more than a woman—8 st 5 lb. Temu is much the same height, 5 ft $7\frac{1}{2}$ in., and weighs 9 st 6 lb. There seems to be a lot of truth in the theory that light men make good distance runners. Clarke, of course, disproves this, for he is 5 ft 11 in. and weighs 12 st. I think that this may have been to his disadvantage today, for there is a growing theory that altitude affects the heavy men more than it affects the light men.

At the press conference afterwards Wolde says, graciously: 'Maybe the altitude had something to do with it.' Gammoudi, who is twenty-eight years old and a sergeant-major in the Tunisian Army, says, 'I have beaten them [Temu and Wolde] twice, but they are used to the height. The result today had to do with the altitude.' He can say that again.

The stadium afterwards resembled a casualty-clearing station, with white-coated attendants bending over prone athletes and administering oxygen. But the most pathetic sight of all was the almost lifeless figure of Clarke. He had given everything in pursuit of this gold medal that he so dearly wanted, the gold medal that would silence for ever the critics who say that he cannot win the big race. Eventually, twenty minutes after the race had finished, he had recovered enough to get to his feet, and with one arm round Brian Corrigan and the other arm around the Australian team manager he was virtually carried from the stadium. As they left, Corrigan said something to him and Ron put his head on his friend's shoulder. It is an image that will remain in my memory for many years—the image of these unfair Games.

But let us get back to the other competitions of the afternoon which started with the heats of the 400 metres hurdles. All three British competitors are through to the second round. But I now begin to fear for the chances of Dave Hemery in the finals.

Fifty seconds is not a time that is beaten very often in the 400 metres hurdles, and one certainly does not expect it to be beaten in the heats. But six men ran inside fifty seconds today, and fastest of them all was Ron Whitney who smashed the Olympic record with a time of forty-nine seconds—a time that has only ever been beaten once before and then by Geoff Vanderstock.

John Cooper, the silver medallist in Tokyo, and now, at the age of twenty-eight, a veteran, is third in heat two—won by Juan Dyrzka of the Argentine who has the distinction of being the first man to receive oxygen in these Games.

John Sherwood, the young and powerful Yorkshireman, picked a really tough heat, won by Ron Whitney in 49.0 sec, with Rainer Schubert of West Germany (who set a new European record) second in 49.1 sec and Gary Knoke of Australia third in 49.8 sec. John was fourth in 50.2 sec which equals his best-ever performance.

Dave Hemery, in the fourth heat, came up against the smooth-striding Roberto Frinolli of Italy who won in 49.9 sec with Hemery second in 50.3 sec. Dave says that it felt quite easy. I hope so.

The 800 metres heats are really tough with the first two in each heat, together with the two fastest losers, going through into the next round. At the end of the six heats we are left with only one competitor, twenty-two-year-old Dave Cropper, who won the last heat in the fine time of 1 min 47.9 sec. Chris Carter, the Brighton policeman, who has been handicapped by a tendon injury for the past two weeks, was well below his best, coming sixth in heat four with a time of 1 min 52.9 sec.

Our third competitor in this event, John Davies, did not even start and there is no one who feels it more than young John. He, too, has had a leg injury, and unfortunately there is no expert on athletic injuries amongst the British medical staff. So for three vital days he went without any proper treatment. Eventually he found a tendon expert attached to one of the other teams and managed to get treatment, but it was too late to allow him to run today. You can imagine the heart-break of this nineteen-year-old lad who is so full of promise. He may not have got to the final, but the experience would have been invaluable to him in the coming years. I find it inconceivable that the British Olympic Association should come out here with more than 200 athletes and not bring an expert in physical medicine.

Neither Ron Jones, the British team captain, nor Barrie Kelly had quite enough class to last for very long amongst the world's fastest men. This morning they both got through the first round of the 100 metres, with Kelly recording 10.5 sec and Jones 10.4 sec. But this afternoon, despite running up to their best form, neither could get through to the semi-finals. Ron Jones was sixth in his second-round heat with a time of 10.4 sec and Barrie Kelly was fifth in his heat with a time of 10.3 sec, which equals his personal best. Both Hermes (a good name for a sprinter) Ramirez of Cuba and Charlie Greene of the United States equalled the Olympic record of ten seconds. It is going to be a great final.

One bright domestic spot was the performance of Jeff Teale, the 18 st 8 lb Yorkshireman, in the shot putt. This morning he became the twelfth and last qualifier for the final with 61 ft 11 in., just edging out the European champion Vilmos Varjeu of Hungary by the minute margin of half an inch.

The day ended for me in the Olympic village, where Judy Patching, who, despite his name, is the Australian men's team manager, gave an impromptu press conference in the entrance to the Australian headquarters. 'If Ron Clarke had won twenty gold medals today he could not have brought more honour to himself,' he said. 'He is completely exhausted and under sedation.'

8
'YOU ARE HAPPY JUST TO BE IN THE FINAL OF SUCH A RACE'

Monday, October 14th

'I said before I came here that the world record would go. But I was not expecting to see a 22 ft 4½ in. jump. When she did it I said to myself "Blimey!" and then tried to put it out of my mind.' The speaker was Sheila Sherwood, the twenty-two-year-old Sheffield schoolteacher, better known perhaps as Sheila Parkin, now married to John Sherwood, the 400 metres hurdler. She had just become the first British medal winner of these Games by taking second place in the women's long jump—the event which was won in Tokyo by Mary Rand.

I am told that for a long time this evening the B.B.C. was putting it out over the air that Sheila had won the gold medal. How I wish they had been right! Unfortunately, the Rumanian girl Viorica Viscopoleanu broke the world record (held by Mary Rand) with her very first jump—a distance of 22 ft 4½ in. She did it when the wind, which was blowing against the girls, was absolutely still. Nothing can be so disheartening as for one of your rivals to break the world record with her very first jump. But Sheila Sherwood was not put off. She herself had broken the United Kingdom all-comers' mark with a first jump of 21 ft 7¾ in. This was good enough to put her in third place, behind Viscopoleanu and the Russian girl Tatyana Talysheva, at the end of the third round when the field was reduced to six jumpers. Then with her fifth jump Sheila leapt 21 ft 11 in.—a prodigious leap that gave her the silver medal.

Today is the day when we find out who is the fastest man in

49

the world. The title must lie between two American Negroes, Jim Hines and Charlie Greene—co-holders of the world record at 9.9 sec, the first men to dip under that magic figure of 10 sec for the 100 metres. Jim Hines won the first semi-final this afternoon, equalling Bob Hayes's Olympic record of 10 sec, and Charlie Greene won the second semi-final with a time of 10.1 sec. But do not take too much notice of the times because the wind was absolutely still when Charlie Greene ran but behind Jim Hines when he ran. The most significant thing about the semi-finals was that Charlie Greene's right leg was strapped and he was obviously in pain with his other leg, his left leg, just after he had gone through the tape. He had to be given a whiff of oxygen (after running 100 metres!) and was taken down the ramp to the medical quarters on the arm of one of the attendants. It would be a tragedy if he has pulled a muscle, but it looks to me as if it is nothing worse than cramp.

When they come out for the start of the final I'm busy taking bets. Herb McKenley, who so nearly won this title at Helsinki in 1948 and is now the Jamaican coach, is prepared to put ten pesos (about seven shillings) on his man, Lennox Miller. My colleague, Hugh McIlvanney, puts ten pesos on Charlie Greene and I put the same on Hines. After all, I reckon, Hines has got something to run for—a big, fat contract with an American football team!

It is an electric moment when they get down on to their blocks —the first all-Negro final in Olympic history. In addition to Hines, Miller and Greene, there is the huge Cuban Pablo Montes; the Frenchman from the West Indian island of Martinique, Roger Bambuck; the ancient American Mel Pender (how does he do it at the age of thirty?); the coffee-coloured Canadian Harry Jerome, bronze medallist of Tokyo; and finally the wiry Madagascan, Jean-Louis Ravelomanantsoa.

Mel Pender, his little legs moving so fast that you can hardly see them, it first away, but Hines also has a good start. By the half-distance it looks as if the Americans will get the first three places. But which American will take the title 'The fastest man in the world'?

At three-quarter distance Jim Hines suddenly switches on his supercharger and comes away from the field with an electrifying burst. Behind him Lennox Miller has got up level with Charlie

1 The members and officials of the British Olympic team march round the arena in Mexico City during the opening ceremonies of the XIXth Olympic Games

2 Enriqueta Basilio carries the Olympic torch up the 90 steps to the Olympic flame cauldron during the opening ceremony of the Olympics in Mexico City

3 *Above:* Sheila Sherwood of Great Britain jumped 21 feet 11 inches to win England's first medal, a silver, in the women's long jump

4 *Below:* David Hemery clears the final hurdle on his way to a gold medal and a new world record of 48.1 seconds in the final of the 400 metres hurdles

5 *Above:* Jim Hines of United States wins the final of the 100 metres with a world and Olympic record of 9.9 seconds. Lennox Miller of Jamaica is second and Charlie Green of United States is third

6 *Below:* Great Britain's David Hemery waves at the jubilant crowd after receiving his gold medal. John Sherwood, who won a bronze medal in the 400 metres hurdles, is on his left

7 Randy Matson, here in action, hurled the 16 lb. ball 67 ft 4¾ in. to capture the gold medal for United States

8 The Netherlands four-man team here *en route* to victory in the 100 kilometres time-trial. Sweden was second and Italy third

9 Tommie Smith of United States throws up his arms as he wins the 200 metres in a world record time of 19.8 seconds. Michael Fray of Jamaica is on the right and John Carlos of United States on the left

10 Bob Seagren of United States clears the bar in the final of the pole vault with a jump of 17 ft 8½ in. which gave him the gold medal

11 Disappointment for Lillian Board of Great Britain as she comes in second to win the silver medal in the 400 metres for women. She was overtaken at the last moment by Collette Besson of France

12 The field in the 50 kilometres walk strides around the track at the Olympic stadium before heading out on to the streets of Mexico City

3 Willie Davenport of United States throws up his arms as he finishes the 110 metres hurdles equalling the Olympic record of 13.3 seconds

4 Yanis Lusis hurls the javelin over 295 ft to win the gold medal for U.S.S.R.

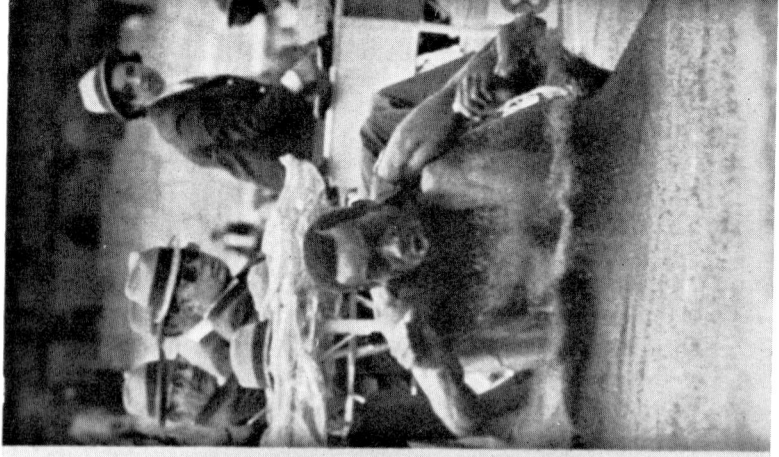

Opposite page:

15 Bob Beamon of United States sails to a new world record of 29 ft 2½ in. in the men's long jump. The photograph in the centre shows his landing as he sprays sand in front of him and in right photograph he struggles to maintain his balance after rising

16 Gyula Zsivotzky of Hungary set a new Olympic record in the hammer with a throw of 240 ft 8 in. Here he is seen in action in the qualifying round

17 'The Fosbury Flop'— this is the unconventional style used by Dick Fosbury of the United States in the high jump which carried him to an Olympic gold medal

18 *Above:* Kipchoge Keino of Kenya wins the 1500 metres final in a new Olympic record time of 3 minutes 34.9 seconds. Fifteen yards behind in second place is world record holder Jim Ryun of United States

19 *Below:* Jim Hines (extreme right) takes the baton from Ronnie Smith in the 4 × 100 metres relay and runs to a new world record time of 38.2 seconds bringing United States a gold medal

20 *Above:* Great Britain's *Superdocious* leads U.S.S.R.'s *Nayada* in the Flying Dutchman class. The British crew Rodney Pattison and Ian Macdonald-Smith won the gold medal in this event winning 5 of the 7 races

21 *Below:* Members of Great Britain's equestrian team display their gold medals at the conclusion of the three-day event. Left to right: Maj. Derek S. Allhusen, Jane Bullen, Richard J. H. Meade, and S/Sgt. R. S. Jones

22 *Above:* World record holder Debbie Meyer of United States sets a new Olympic record of 2 minutes, 10.5 seconds to win the women's 200 metres free-style final

23 *Below:* Lajos Szucs, on his way to scoring Hungary's fifth goal against Japan in their semi-final in the soccer competition

24 Ingehorg Busch of West Germany dives from the highboard during an early round of the diving competition

25 Mexico's first gold medal as Felipe Munoz just beats world record holder Vladimir Kosinsky in the 200 metres breaststroke final

26 Marion Coakes of Great Britain on Stroller, here in action in the preliminary round, took a silver medal in the individual jumping competition

27 Russian and Yugoslav players scramble for the ball during a basketball semi-final which Yugoslavia won 63–62

28 *Above:* Jean Allemand of France tumbles off the platform during the épée finals in a fencing match against Gianluigi Saccaro of Italy

29 *Below:* Sharon Wichman of United States, nearest, overtakes Russia's Galina Prozumenshikova during the final of the 200 metres breaststroke. Miss Wichman went on to win the gold medal

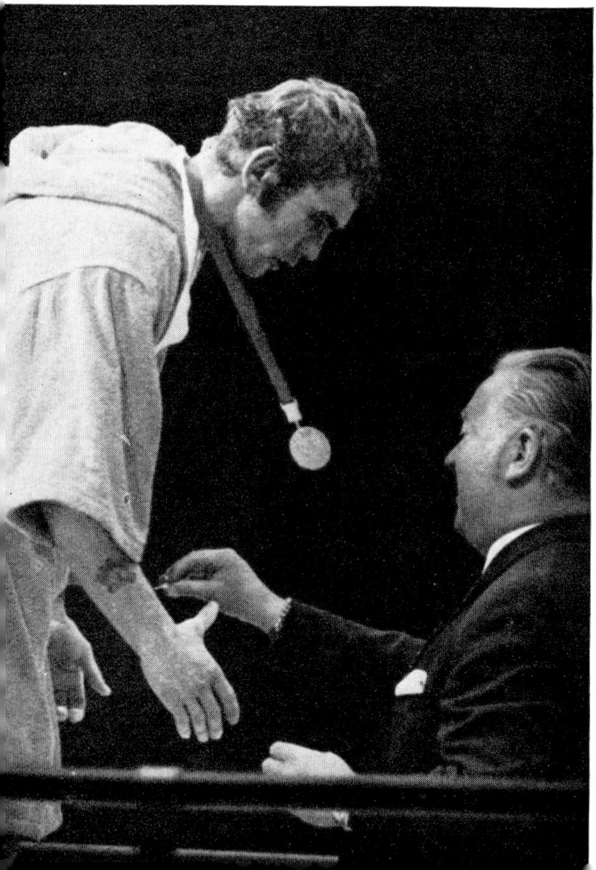

30 Tibor Tatai of Hungary (5) wins the Canadian Singles canoe race in a close finish with West Germany's Detlef Lewe (2)

31 Christopher Finnegan of Great Britain shakes hands with Lord Killanin after being awarded the gold medal for his victory over Kiseliov of Russia in the middleweight boxing final

Greene and just beats him by dipping for the tape. The time for Hines is 9.9 sec, a new Olympic record and equalling the world record. In fact, the electrical timing apparatus shows that it was really 9.89 sec, and I am sure that this is the fastest 100 metres the world has ever seen by a good yard. As far as I know, the timing of the race in Sacramento in California earlier this year, when Charlie Greene and Jim Hines broke the world record, was by hand, and hand timing nearly always gives a faster time than electrical timing for the simple reason that the finger on the stop-watch button is slow at the start and tends to anticipate the finish. So by hand timing I reckon Hines might have been given 9.8 sec.

At the press conference afterwards Hines says that his record 'Might be broken at any time—the way sprinters are going.' Jim is twenty-two, 6 ft tall and weighs 12 st 12 lb. He was born in Arkansas but is now a student at Texas Southern University in Houston. He is married with one child, a daughter. Lennox Miller, of Jamaica, is also twenty-two, 5 ft 11 in. tall and 11 st 11 lb. He goes to university in America—to the University of Southern California in Los Angeles. Charlie Greene is the oldest and smallest of this incredible trio—he is twenty-four, 5 ft 8 in. tall and weighs 10 st 12 lb—a good weight for a middle-distance runner.

When Hines is asked when he will sign professional forms for the Miami Dolphins, a new football club, he says, 'First we have got to get together—if you know what that means.' Everybody does know what it means—that his win today will put his price up considerably. One American journalist told me that his contract may bring him in a total of half a million dollars, but other American journalists say that this is nonsense, that the days of the mammoth contracts are over. Apparently Bob Hayes, the winner of the 100 metres in Tokyo, now plays for the Dallas Texans and gets 45,000 to 50,000 dollars every year. They reckon that Jim Hines will be worth about 35,000 to 50,000 dollars per year to the Miami Dolphins.

People often ask why the Americans manage to retain such supremacy in sprinting—since the early thirties American athletes have won both the sprint titles at all the Olympics except for Rome in 1960 where the West German, Armin Hary, won the 100 metres and Livio Berruti of Italy won the 200 metres. There is no simple answer, but I think it is a combination of the fact that they have almost perfect weather for sprinting in the western half of the States, that the competition tends to be very fierce, and that there are great incentives, especially for the black Americans, who find it much easier to get a university education if they are also good at sport. And when you add to this the incentive of an American football contract, which will provide a meal ticket for life, I do not find it so surprising that they are so good.

Jesse Owens, whom Jim Hines graciously calls 'the greatest track and field athlete in the history of America—one of my heroes,' explains this upsurge in sprint times by saying, 'They (the athletes) are bigger, stronger and faster than my generation. Also the competition is fiercer. And inventions such as the tartan track make a difference too.' The altitude also makes a difference to these men in the explosive events because some recent research has shown that a 100 metres runner expends about 20 per cent of his energy on overcoming the air resistance. So, if the air resistance is less because of the altitude, it follows that times should be faster. But it is really impossible to say exactly how much effect this has in terms of time. And it is also impossible to say how much improvement comes from the tartan track. But it stands to reason that an absolutely consistent track in which the spike cannot leave a pot-hole is faster than the conventional cinders.

Charlie Greene confirms that his trouble in the semi-final was cramp: 'I started to get it at about ninety metres. The semi-final really is the toughest race. The tension is so great that you are very unsure of yourself. You say to yourself, "If only I can get past this one." I don't think the spectators realise how happy you are just to be in the final of such a race.'

From the sublime 100 metres, let us descend to the ridiculous 3000 metres steeplechase. I call it ridiculous because the altitude has reduced it to a farce. At sea-level one would expect the winner's time to be somewhere between 8 min 20 sec and 8 min 30 sec. To-day, in the heats, only two men managed to get below nine minutes, and both of them are highland athletes—Benjamin Kojo of Kenya, who won the first heat in 8 min 57.8 sec, and another Kenyan, nineteen-year-old Amos Biwott, who won the third heat in 8 min 49.4 sec. Biwott is the most incredible find of these games. He has never taken part in the steeplechase before this year. According to the Kenyan team manager, Biwott failed to qualify in the 5000 metres in his district sports, so he switched, the same afternoon, to the steeplechase. He managed to win and went on to the district championships and thus into the Kenyan Olympic team. He cannot hurdle and he takes the water jump with a fabulous explosion of energy—accelerating into it and then doing a mighty hitch kick off the bar so that he completely clears the water. There is a current story that someone has given him a new pair of spikes which he wants to take home with him and he says that water won't do them any good!

The sad thing is that Britain has not one competitor in the final, and this is the first time that this has happened since steeplechasing was first taken seriously in Britain by John Disley and his coach, Geoff Dyson, in 1950. Our three competitors are capable of times of 8 min 30 sec at sea-level, but today John Jackson is knocked out in 9 min 11.4 sec, Gareth Bryan-Jones is knocked out in 9 min 16.8 sec, and Maurice Herriott is carried away on a stretcher after running 9 min 33.0 sec—and this is the man that won the silver medal in Tokyo.

In my diary of the 1964 Games I criticised Maurice for his tactics in the steeplechase. I thought that he should have kept closer to Gaston Roelants, the eventual winner, instead of hanging back and being satisfied with coming through to take the silver medal. But I am now regretting that criticism, for there is no man in the British team who has given more loyal service or who has run so often until his heart is fit to burst.

Today I felt like throttling the whole of the International Olympic Committee when Maurice was carried off on a stretcher, his hand trailing, lifelessly, on the track. He cannot remember the last two laps—indeed he cannot even remember finishing. He himself regrets that this, his last race before he is going to retire, should end this way. And so do I. You can ask so much of a man, and Herriott was asked, by the International Olympic Committee who chose Mexico City, to do an unnatural, inhuman thing—to run over twenty-eight hurdles and seven water jumps for nearly two miles in this pitifully thin air. Those who say that the problems of running at altitude are 'all in the mind', and that they are not nearly as bad as has been made out, should remember Maurice Herriott. In the next two days he was to black out on three or four occasions. On the morning after his race he was not even able to get to the lavatory without assistance. Jim Hogan helped him there and then Maurice said that he would be all right. But Jim tells me that Maurice then had to call for assistance before he could get back to his bed. Are the athletes of all nations assembled here 'in fair and equal competition'? I have asked that question before and I expect I will ask it again before the Games are over.

You may gather from all this that I have not exactly enjoyed today's athletics and you would be dead right. How can one enjoy a sport in which many of the men whom you admire are tested so unnaturally and carried out of the stadium on stretchers? Thankfully, the prospect for tomorrow is much better. We are now down to the finalists in the 400 metres hurdles and the 800 metres, and they both promise to be great races.

In the first semi-final of the 400 metres hurdles John Sherwood broke the United Kingdom National and Commonwealth record with a time of 49.3 sec—and that is nearly a second, nine-tenths of a second to be exact, off his previous best. Truly, the Olympics bring out the best in some people. Yet such a time was only good enough for third place, with Frinolli of Italy winning in 49.2 sec and Geoff Vanderstock of America second, also in 49.2 sec. In the same semi-final John Cooper, hero of Tokyo, just did not have enough speed and was eliminated with a time of 50.8 sec.

A few minutes later Dave Hemery equalled John Sherwood's record, even though he was only putting out his maximum effort for the first half of the race. His semi-final was won by Gerhard Hennige, the West German, in 49.1 sec with Ron Whitney second in 49.2 sec and Dave Hemery third in 49.3 sec. What a phenomenal final it is going to be.

And what a final the 800 metres will be. Today a competitor had to break 1 min 47.0 sec to get into the final. Surprisingly, neither of the semi-finals was won by an altitude man, although Thomas Saisi of Kenya took the field in the first semi-final through the 400 metres in an electrifying 51.5 sec. But he could not hold this pace, and both Walter Adams of West Germany and Dieter Fromm of East Germany went past him in the finishing straight for times of 1 min 46.4 sec and 1 min 46.5 sec respectively.

In the second semi-final Wilson Kiprugut, the Kenyan soldier, and the Tokyo bronze medallist, shot into the lead and passed the bell in 51.3 sec with at least ten yards on the next runner.

Kiprugut was still in the lead when they came into the final straight, but gradually Ralph Doubell, the twenty-three-year-old Australian, who had been last at the bell, worked his way through the field and overtook Kiprugut with a strong finish. This man Doubell is another of the revelations of the Games. I have heard a lot about him because he is trained by Franz Stampfl, who was coach to Roger Bannister, Chris Chataway, Brian Hewson, Jean Desforges (who is now Mrs. Ron Pickering), and myself before he emigrated to Australia in 1955 to take up a post in Melbourne University. Franz has always prophesied that Doubell would be a great athlete one day. It looks as though his prophecy is going to come true.

Dave Cropper, the last surviving Englishman, was last in this second semi-final, but that is no disgrace for his time was 1 min 47.6 sec, which is faster than he has ever run before this year. Some people wonder whether it is worth sending athletes who are going to come last in the semi-final or perhaps be knocked out in the very first heat. My answer is that if they are young then it is absolutely essential to send them to the Olympics for there is nothing like Olympic experience to hone a man and give him the steely quality which he needs in all international competitions these days. Dave Cropper is only twenty-two years old and his best running is still to come.

This gloomy day was lightened in the last final of the afternoon —the twenty kilometres walk, the event which was won by Ken Matthews in 1964. This year we didn't really expect our trio, Arthur Jones, John Webb and Bob Hughes, to get amongst the medals, but Arthur Jones certainly had a go at keeping with the leaders for the first quarter of the race. The first man into the stadium at the end of an hour and a half's walking was the thirty-two-year-old Russian Vladimir Golubnichiy, who won this event in the 1960 Games at Rome and who came third behind Ken Matthews in Tokyo. Twenty yards behind him came his teammate Nickolay Smaga and then, five seconds later, the stadium exploded. There in third place, making up ground fast, was Mexico's outstanding hope of a gold medal in the track and field events, the thirty-one-year-old soldier José Pedraza. I am not enough of a walking expert to accuse Señor Pedraza of running, but it certainly seemed to be very odd that he could go down the back straight almost twice as fast as such an experienced walker as Smaga. The judges looked at him askance, but no man would have the courage to disqualify Pedraza in front of 60,000 or 70,000 of his screaming compatriots.

He streaked past Smaga and then closed right up to Golubnichiy, but now in the finishing straight the judges were there with their red and white flags and Pedraza had to ease back into a walk while Golubnichiy strolled on for the gold medal in a time of one hour 33 min 58.4 sec—over four and a half minutes slower than Ken Matthews' winning time in Tokyo.

As Señor Pedraza crossed the finishing line having won a silver medal (which I am not certain he deserved) he shook his fists at himself and held his head in his hands. He was almost suicidal with rage at himself for not having kept closer to the leaders and so given himself an opportunity of the gold medal (he was thirty-five seconds behind Golubnichiy and Smaga at the fifteen kilometres mark). An attendant went up to him and threw a blanket over his shoulders, but Pedraza tore it off and threw it on the ground—and went on cursing himself for a full five minutes. It shows the right spirit. For some competitors, the truly great ones, a silver or a bronze medal is not enough. Only a gold is good enough at the Olympic Games. Only a gold satisfies that longing to prove yourself the best in the world.

9
'THERE ARE A THOUSAND HILLS AND SAND-DUNES BEHIND YOU...'

Tuesday, October 15th

This afternoon I stood on my seat at the Olympic Stadium and went berserk. As far as I know I was shouting: 'What supremacy! What unbelievable supremacy!'

There, on the tartan track, a tall blonde Englishman, Dave Hemery, was streaking towards the tape with a lead that seemed like forty yards but was in fact about eight yards. But eight yards over the world-record holder, the European champion and five other great 400 metres hurdlers is an almost undreamt of margin.

When I recovered my equilibrium I said to a member of the National Union of Track Statisticians: 'There cannot ever have been such a margin of superiority in an Olympic final.' You can't say that to a NUT without being disproved and sure enough he came up with the answer that, in Tokyo, both Bob Hayes in the 100 metres and Abebe Bikila in the marathon had won by margins which on a percentage basis were greater. But what company to keep! Hayes, the greatest sprinter that I have ever seen; Bikila, the only man to have won the Olympic marathon title on two successive occasions; and Dave Hemery, Britain's first gold medallist of these Games.

Let's go back to the start of the race. The line up from the inside reads like this: Rainer Schubert, of West Germany, the co-holder of the European record at 49.1 sec; Gerhard Hennige, also of West Germany and also the co-holder of the European record at 49.1 sec—the man who had looked so impressive in both his heats and his semi-finals; Geoff Vanderstock, the young twenty-two-year-old American who broke the world record with a time of 48.8 sec in the U.S. Olympic trials at Lake Tahoe; Roberto Frinolli of Italy, the European champion; Viacheslav Shomarokhov, the twenty-eight-year-old Russian who is a deaf mute; then Dave Hemery, twenty-four, 6 ft 1$\frac{1}{2}$ in. tall, born in Cirencester in Gloucestershire and graduate of Boston University in the United States; then Ron Whitney, holder of the Olympic record, at 49.0 sec, and regarded by many people as the greatest 400 metres hurdler in the world. Finally on the outside John Sherwood, powerful, twenty-three years old and co-holder with Hemery of the Commonwealth and U.K. record at 49.3 sec. I have not looked it up, but I can say without any fear of contradiction that there has never been a final in this event in which all eight men have been under 50 sec.

I could not get all the runners into the field of my binoculars at the start, so I concentrated on the outside three runners—two Englishmen with Whitney, the favourite, sandwiched in between. Hemery got a good start and took the first hurdle as if it didn't exist. There was just an imperceptible rising of the blonde head as he strode over it. Then again the imperceptible rise for the second hurdle. And now I couldn't believe my eyes. He had already caught up the stagger on Ron Whitney and that stagger is supposed to last for two bends. There is an old cliché about a runner 'eating up the ground'. But that is the only description for Hemery as he went down the back straight.

Now I began to fear for him. Was he 'blowing' his chances by going too fast in the first 200 metres? Would he be able to hang on in that long final straight when the lack of oxygen would begin to affect his legs? But there was no hesitation about Hemery. He went on with that long smooth stride, just rising to hurdle after hurdle, changing from thirteen strides to fifteen strides between the hurdles without my noticing. And then he was into the finishing straight. Here at last we would be able to see them on equal terms, but there was nothing equal about this performance. Dave was already six yards up the straight before anybody else left the bend. Now I, like every other Briton in the stadium, was on my feet, cheering him home, not believing the evidence of my own eyes, the evidence that showed that he was pulverising this field into oblivion.

I have much sympathy for David Coleman, who said, during his commentary on B.B.C. television, 'Who cares about third.' I did not see who was second or third or fourth or fifth. All I saw was Hemery first and the rest nowhere.

Others, more calm, reported that John Sherwood had come through in the last few yards to snatch the bronze medal. I dashed round to the ramp, down which the athletes enter the stadium, to find, and congratulate, Hemery, but he had been carried off to the medical centre to give his 'sample' so that the medical men could test for dope. In a way I am rather glad that there are these tests because some idiot would only start to query Dave's fabulous margin of superiority. There, on the ground just outside the stadium, was John Sherwood, flat on his back, completely exhausted. He could not believe that he had come third and, indeed, at that moment, it didn't seem to matter whether it was third or fourth for he had the satisfaction of knowing that he had given everything to the race.

At last the times went up on the electric scoreboard. First, Hemery, Great Britain, 48.1 sec, a new Olympic and world record. At the beginning of this year the record stood at 49.1 sec (Rex Crawley of the United States, set in Los Angeles in 1964). Then, just a month ago, Geoff Vanderstock brought it down to 48.8 sec at the United States Olympic trials at Lake Tahoe. Now Dave Hemery has knocked another incredible seven-tenths of a second off that record. So in the space of two months it has come down by a full second and such a thing has not happened since the days of Glenn Hardin who knocked 1.1 sec off Bob Tisdall's unofficial time of 51.7 sec. But that was way back in 1934.

But let us go back to that scoreboard. Second, Hennige, West Germany, 49.0 sec; third, Sherwood, Great Britain, 49.0 sec; fourth, Vanderstock, United States 49.0 sec; fifth, Skomarokhov, Russia, 49.1 sec; sixth, Whitney, United States, 49.2 sec; seventh, Schubert, West Germany, 49.2 sec. All these broke the previous Olympic record. Only Frinolli, of Italy, was outside the previous record, and he was eighth in 50.1 sec.

Before I dwell at length on Dave Hemery let me make a tribute to John Sherwood. Inevitably his performance is overshadowed by Hemery's gold medal, but we should not forget that he has beaten his previous personal best by the staggering margin of

1.2 sec. He is still only twenty-three and may yet be far from his peak. He has been to the Olympics before but has not competed in them, for he was a reserve for the 4 x 400 metres in Tokyo and never got a run. Some people might think that it was extravagant to send him all the way to Japan, but I am convinced that the experience he got there of mixing with Olympic athletes has helped him to produce the performance which he did today.

Let Hemery relate his own day: 'Last night I managed to get a good sleep because I was very tired. Before the semi-final I had woken up four or five times and had taken an aspirin, but I took nothing before the final today because I didn't want to have anything in my system that might be detrimental. After breakfast I lay down on my bed for about two hours and I was sort of drifting in and out of sleep. I studied the diary which I had pinned up on the wall of my room which shows in detail the last seven months of my training. I wanted to remind myself of all the work that I had put in, trying to win the gold medal. And I reminded myself of a letter which my coach, Billy Smith of Boston, had sent me. He said: "There are a thousand hills and sand-dunes behind you and there isn't time for the others to catch up."

'I've done fifty-nine weeks of training without a break. Smithie is always trying to bolster my confidence—to tell me what I'll do this time. I never believe him but he always turns out to be right.

'The worst time in the whole day was when we got down to the track and I still had about two hours to go before my race. It was much too early to start warming up and I spent an hour in the medical centre with Denis Watts, John Cooper, and John Sherwood. It is a strange feeling. You want to go through with the race and yet at the same time you don't want to go through with it. The mind is a weird contraption. Once I started warming up I felt better. I warmed up very carefully, trying to recover completely between each exercise. And then I lay down for ten minutes while Whitney was jogging away on my right. It was a very tense time. I wasn't feeling terribly strong and I kept on trying to get as much oxygen as possible into the system.

'When I went on to the track I was trying to think of what I could run for a flat quarter, but I was in a strange sort of limbo state. I was thinking: "Am I warm enough to run as fast as I have ever done in my life." There were a lot of Americans shouting,

"Come on Ron." I tried not to think of them. I knew that I had to do the first 200 metres in 22.8 to 23.2 sec, dependent on the weather. As you know, it wasn't very good weather. I thought that the wet would make it nearer 23.2. After twenty yards I felt I was going well—running fast but relaxed. I wanted to overhaul Whitney early on and then I had my eye on John, trying to catch him by the fifth flight. I had been a little undecided before the race as to whether I should try to go to the seventh flight before changing my strides from thirteen to fifteen between the flights, but because of the weather I decided to change after six. Then I started to work the chop down very hard—to try to get my feet on the ground quickly after each hurdle. I told myself to relax again.

'It's funny how the mind ticks over like this. Just before or just after the eighth hurdle I heard a step on the inside of me, splashing in the water. Then I put in a lot of effort. I remembered my coach telling me to go at the tenth hurdle as if it is the first hurdle in a high hurdles race. Then I was over it and trying to sprint, but I wasn't satisfied with the speed. I can remember my mind yelling at myself to get sprinting and yet I couldn't. I was scared to death. Worried about Whitney's finish. After the line I looked right to see where Whitney was. The only thing I had been worried about was getting enough lead to hold them off in the finish. But when I looked to the right there was no one there.

'I felt pretty rough afterwards. I almost blacked out once or twice. I suppose I must have put my hands on my knees and held on about twenty times. There wasn't any great elation perhaps because of the fatigue. I was just happy to have done what I thought I could do.

'Of course they wanted a urine sample from me for the dope test. But I was so exhausted I couldn't achieve any significant contribution to their cause!'

Dave has lived for fourteen years in Britain and ten years in the States. His family live near Boston, and some people might consider therefore that he is not entirely a 'British' athlete, but such a suggestion would, I suggest, shock Dave, who has managed, despite his American education, to retain an entirely English air. He uses an occasional American expression and delivers it in a slight American accent, but otherwise he is almost a model of the sort of young man who would be picked as a Churchill scholar—a representative abroad of our way of life.

And that is not the sort of person that the British sporting public likes to savour as one of their folk heroes. They seem to fall for the aristocratic, swashbuckling, amateur or for the hard-living, blunt professional, preferably a hard-living Yorkshireman. Which makes me wonder what they, the British public, will make of Hemery now that he has emerged from Mexico as the only gold medallist in the British athletics team.

Yet this is a man who is well worth getting to know. Under the shy, retiring exterior there is a warm and questing human being, sometimes confused in the direction in which he is going yet knowing that he wants to make a mark in life—a mark which will contribute to the betterment of mankind. In the cynical 1950s, that might have sounded like so much sentimental mishmash, but thankfully we no longer seem to be afraid, in the 1960s, of declaring our ideals.

Dave left Britain in 1956 when he was only twelve years old. His father, an accountant, had been asked by an American friend to go out to Colorado Springs and set up an accountancy system for a firm. The job was finished in six months and the family, two girls and two boys, then moved to Boston, one of the only two places in the States which, so Hemery senior was informed, had an education standard that approached that of England.

In 1962 the family emigrated, back to England. Dave was eighteen years old, fresh out of high school and intent on a banking career. He was also a reasonably promising athlete, having been a competent half-miler, quarter-miler and high hurdler at school. One day he went to the Ruislip track with his father, who asked whether there was a reasonable hurdles coach in the area. And so began Dave's association with Fred Housden, a retired Harrow maths master.

Fred Housden is one of those incredible men whom you stumble upon scattered throughout British sport. Some of them coach, some of them keep a club running smoothly, some of them hold watches at meetings and training sessions in winter and in summer. Few are ever heard of, but sport at the recreational and club level collapses without them. Housden, seventy-six years old, is one of the greatest hurdles coaches in the world and a man who is still fit enough to sprint alongside some of our best women hurdlers (Pat Pryce and Maxime Botley, for instance), urging them to greater effort.

In that summer of 1962 he taught Dave Hemery how to hurdle, converting him, in the space of three months, from a 15.6 sec performer over schoolboy hurdles to a 14.7 sec performer over the full man-sized hurdles—a conversion that normally adds tenths of seconds to an athlete's time. Dave still goes to Fred Housden for advice and regards him, equally with Billy Smith of Boston, as his coach.

Dave was now working in the Westminster Bank, but not for very long. His young brother and sister, both thoroughly Americanised, were finding it impossible to settle down in England. They would be greeted at school with taunts of 'Go home, Yank'. Once again this close-knit family pulled up its English roots and returned to Boston. For a year Dave worked in a Boston bank and that is the last we would have heard of him if it had not been for a week's holiday which he took with his brother John in Bermuda in the spring of 1964.

The holiday unsettled him, made him realise that there was more to life than sitting at the desk pushing a pencil from nine till five. He wanted to travel, to meet people—to become an airline pilot, perhaps. But his eyesight was not good enough (he wears contact lenses for hurdling). Instead he chose aeronautical engineering at Boston University, but soon decided that the life of an engineer was often a closed life, behind a desk, pushing the figures around.

He then switched to the international business course, wide-ranging and a worth-while background for many careers. The international law section of the course interested him greatly and he thought of becoming an international lawyer. 'But you have to be unfeeling to be a lawyer. Devoid of anything . . . How shall I put it—cold and calculating perhaps. You can't get emotionally involved in a case. The side of me that wants to help others would be frustrated.'

He is still in search of a career. He thought of teaching, but was shocked to find that many people use it as an easy way out because they feel they cannot make the grade elsewhere. 'That is disaster, to my way of thinking,' he says.

With the American population getting younger every year (by 1970, 50 per cent of Americans will be under twenty-five years old), he sees the desperate need for using the best teachers more effectively. And that is the field that he will go into once the Olympics are over—research into new methods of mass education.

It was Billy Smith of Boston who suggested that he could make a better 400 metres hurdler than high hurdler, an art which requires tremendous basic speed. Hemery, on the other hand, has always been tremendously strong. In the indoor meets he has recently run the 600 yards, 1000 yards and a leg of the relay in the same evening.

This year all his work has been concentrated on strength. The first time he saw a hurdle was in April. 'It was quite refreshing, the quarter hurdles seemed almost short.' And yet the quarter hurdles are often described as the man-killer amongst the track events.

Some weeks before the Games I asked him if he would be disappointed if he did not win the gold medal. He said: 'It sounds awful to say, but I will be disappointed with anything less than the gold. To many people it sounds very big-headed. But, yes, I would be.'

If he did not have such an attitude he would not have won today, for he is not a hater of his opponents or even a hater of himself. He simply 'hates the thought of getting beaten—horrible thought'.

As an illustration of the sort of work that is necessary for an athlete to aspire to a gold medal let me tell the story of one day last winter when Dave Hemery descended to the basement of the thirteen-floor dormitory building which he inhabits on the campus of Boston University. Normally, every afternoon, Dave changed in the sparse headquarters of the university athletic team, a basement room, and then went out to train on the wooden track which is laid outdoors on the football field. On this day, however, he had no thought of changing. The temperature outside was far below freezing and the wind and the snow were combining into a blizzard. In the basement he met Billy Smith, the part-time coach to Boston University. Smith opened the door on to the swirling snow and said, 'The road to Mexico is out there. . . .'

But we must get back into the Olympic Stadium, to the final

of the 800 metres. At lunchtime today I went down to the Olympic village with Franz Stampfl because he wanted to talk to Ron Clarke about the heats of the 5000 metres. Nobody could really expect Ron to start in the 5000 metres after his traumatic experience just two days ago. Surely he has punished his body enough. But Ron is determined to have another attempt at winning that precious gold medal even though, in his heart, he must know that the altitude will beat him.

Normally a man of Clarke's ability would take it easy in the heat, conserving himself for the final, but Stampfl knew that Clarke was suffering from a greater hurt to his mind than to his body. So he advised him to go out in the last three laps and pile on the pressure. Those in the room, including Ralph Doubell, who later in the afternoon was competing in the 800 metres final, agreed. But as Stampfl and I left the village, Brian Corrigan, the doctor, ran after him. 'You can't ask him to do that, Franz. You will kill him,' said Corrigan. Stampfl asked Corrigan if he really believed that Clarke would injure himself physically. 'Because if you do,' said Stampfl, 'you must tell him not to run. But if he is physically fit to run then he must do it this way.'

Stampfl did not have to tell Doubell what tactics to adopt in the 800 metres. They were obvious. One, or both, of the two Kenyans, Kiprugut and Saisi, would go out and run the first lap in about fifty-one seconds. Doubell had to stay somewhere near the back of the field and then to work his way through until he could come off the final bend with that tremendous finish of his and hope to catch Kiprugut on the tape. And so it happened.

The young and inexperienced Saisi didn't give Kiprugut any help, so the Tokyo bronze medallist had to go out on his own, and a very good job he made of it, going through the 400 metre mark in fifty-one seconds with a good seven yards lead over Benedict Cayenne of Trinidad. Doubell was towards the back of the field and Tom Farrell, the American who also has a good finish, was last. Down the back straight the Kenyan was still striding out in front and I wondered whether Doubell could really catch him. But the Australian was making his way cunningly through the field and went into the final bend some seven yards behind Kiprugut.

As Doubell came into the finishing straight I knew that he

would catch Kiprugut for he unleashed a sprint of which both Bannister or Brian Hewson would have been proud. He caught Kiprugut some forty yards from the tape and then the Kenyan held on gamely to finish a yard back. Doubell's time was an astonishing 1 min 44.3 sec, which equals Peter Snell's world record. Kiprugut recorded 1 min 44.5 sec, with Tom Farrell winning the bronze medal with 1 min 45.4 sec.

Such fast times make many people believe that altitude does not affect the 800 metres, but I think they should ask Noel Carroll that question. It certainly affected him in the heats. I believe that we saw a performance today that was about a second faster than Snell's world record. Certainly it is the greatest 800 metres I have ever seen.

I have run out of superlatives today and yet I still have to report the performance of Mr. Al Oerter, aged thirty-two, a supervisor of the computer communications department at the Grumman Aircraft Engineering Corporation, who lives with his wife and children on Long Island, New York. Al Oerter won the gold medal for the discus at Melbourne in 1956, at Rome in 1960 and in Tokyo in 1964. Nobody expected him to win here, for his best ever performance is just over 207 ft, whereas his compatriot, Jay Silvester, has taken the world record up to 224 ft 5 in. this year. But, as Oerter says himself, 'There is a special inspiration at the Olympics'. There must be because today Al Oerter became the first man to win a gold medal in four successive Olympics and he did it despite a slipped disc which causes him considerable pain and forces him to wear a surgical collar. Today he took the collar off. 'These are the Olympics,' he says. 'You die for them.'

Al won with his third throw which went 212 ft 6 in.—five feet further than he has ever thrown before. What an incredible competitor this man is! There is a considerable body of opinion that regards his performance today as the greatest we have seen so far in the Olympics. They point out that no one else has won four gold medals in a row. But I cannot agree with them. In the track events there are thousands, tens of thousands, of athletes vying for a place in their Olympic team and then for the gold medal. But the discus is a very esoteric event. At a rough guess I do not believe that there could be more than a thousand serious discus throwers in the whole world. So I do not think you can compare the performance of a discus-thrower, even one who has won his event at four successive games, with one or two of the most outstanding gold medallists in the track events. Nevertheless, this should not detract from a quality about this man Oerter which is common to all sporting endeavour. One of the arts in sport is to bring yourself to a peak at the right time and without doubt the champion of that art is Al Oerter.

I have only got time for a quick look at the women's event, but Wyomia Tyus' performance in winning the women's 100 metres final for the second time must not go unrecorded. She has become the first athlete, male or female, to win a sprint title in two successive Olympics. There was no doubt about her victory today, for she dominated the race just as Hines had done in the men's 100 metres. Her time of eleven seconds broke the world record which she holds with three other girls and, of course, it broke her own Olympic record. It was pouring with rain for her race and it was pouring when she went out to collect her medal. When she came into the press conference afterwards she said she was 'a very wet Tigerbelle'—Tigerbelle being the name of her club. She said: 'This will be my last Olympics, I am going to hang up my shoes afterwards. I've been in track for ten years and I'm not getting any younger. It's time I gave up.' When asked whether her record would last for long she said, 'No. Next year or next week it will be broken.'

Neither of the two British girls, Della James and Val Peat, managed to survive the semi-finals, although Della James ran very creditably to record 11.6 sec. On the other hand, we have two girls in the final of the women's 400 metres—Janet Simpson, who came third in her semi-final with a time of 54.0 sec, and Lillian Board, who won the second semi-final in 52.5 sec. I do not know why, but I am worried about tomorrow. Lillian Board looks just too much of a certainty to win the gold medal and I never like certainties in the Olympics.

However, I will prophesy one thing with absolute certainty. Ron Clarke will not win the 5000 metres. Today he ran his heat exactly as he planned. With three laps to go he started to hot up the pace, but little Naftali Temu, of Kenya, the man who won the 10,000 metres, went with him and with supreme confidence ran on Clarke's shoulder for the whole of those last three laps as if saying, 'Come on, try and leave me'.

Sad to relate, all three British competitors are out of the 5000 metres. Dick Taylor, who has had to struggle for fitness ever since he was involved in a car accident in June, came eighth in his heat (won by Kipchoge Keino in 14 min 28.4 sec) with a time of 14 min 46.6 sec. Alan Blinston was seventh in his heat (won by Temu in 14 min 20.4 sec) with a time of 15 min 6.2 sec. And Allan Rushmer was eighth in his heat (won by Wadoux of France in 14 min 19.8 sec) with a time of 15 min 5.2 sec. This is the first time in my recollection (and I have been at every Olympics since 1952) that Britain has not been represented in the final of the 5000 metres. But then we are a lowland nation and we have abided by the altitude-training rules.

By far the most enjoyable day of the Games so far ended pleasantly with a reunion dinner for Franz Stampfl's pupils. Roger Bannister, Chris Chataway, Ralph Doubell, Tony Sneazwell, Allen Crawley (these last three are Australians) and myself gathered with Franz in a private room in a restaurant in Mexico City and chewed the cud over the old days and savoured Ralph Doubell's victory with him. I suppose it was predictable that Franz would gather the same sort of people around him in Melbourne as he did in London. They regard their athletics as only one facet of a full life—and that is as it should be.

10
'IF I DO SOMETHING GOOD THEN I AM AN AMERICAN, BUT IF I DO SOMETHING BAD THEN I AM A NEGRO'

Wednesday, October 16th

It is very hard on a girl of nineteen who wins an Olympic silver medal that she should be regarded as a disappointment to her countrymen. But those are the facts of life.

Lillian Board, the nineteen-year-old Ealing typist, broke her own United Kingdom national record with a time of 52.1 sec and won the silver medal today—yet this is regarded as failure. The whole trouble is that we all expected her to win the gold medal. I still believe that she is the most talented runner in the field today, but she is young, inexperienced in this class of competition, and she was jittering with nerves.

I feared for her when she came out to the start, because she put her spikes on and then took them off again, and then she took off her tracksuit before anyone else, and then when she realised that the others were still fiddling around she picked up her tracksuit top and wrapped it round her thighs to try to preserve some warmth. It was not easy for her because the start was delayed for twenty minutes for some unknown reason, and those twenty minutes could have served only to build up the tension inside her. When, eventually, the officials were ready and the other competitors were ready, she stood behind her blocks, brushed her short hair back behind her ears, fiddled with her shorts, brushed her hair back yet again, licked her lips, touched her face. I don't think I've seen anyone quite so nervous at the start of any race.

She was in the inside lane and so could see all her competitors outside her. She started well, but there was a tightness about her running that I have never noticed before. She was really pushing it round the final bend and now let her tell the story: 'Coming into the straight, I found myself in the lead. I could not believe it, I thought it couldn't last . . . and it didn't.' I wonder what would have happened if she had believed that she could hold that lead? But I do not suppose it would have made much difference because her trouble was that she was so very tight, so unrelaxed.

To us, watchers in the stand, that finishing straight seemed interminable. When she came into the straight, Lillian had three to four yards lead, but gradually the girls behind her started to close up, and suddenly from amongst them we noticed the dark, flowing hair of the French girl, Colette Besson, overhauling Lillian, coming past her and going into the lead in those last few and vital yards.

Before the race you could not have got any odds at all on Colette Besson winning—not even from a French journalist. Yet her time of 52.0 sec equalled the Olympic record set by Betty Cuthbert in 1964. Lillian was a yard back, perhaps less, with a time of 52.1 sec and the Russian girl, Natalia Pechenkina, third in 52.2 sec.

In fourth place, and it was almost as much of a surprise as Colette Besson's win, was Janet Simpson in 52.5 sec. Janet seems far too small and too pretty to be a 400 metres runner. She is, of course, better known for her sprinting. It was only this year that she switched properly to the 400 metres. Before the race she had been in tears because on this day, of all days, she had caught a heavy cold and felt that she would not be able to do herself justice. She has not really done the stamina training that a 400 metres runner needs. If she ever trains for the distance I am sure we shall see some electrifying performances.

Lillian was very gracious at the press conference afterwards. When asked if she thought she could have won she said, 'Colette ran faster than I did today.' She made no excuses for herself and I am not going to make any for her. Mlle Besson, a twenty-two-year-old physical education teacher from the South of France, near Bordeaux, was better than Lillian today because she managed to keep calm.

Lillian, of course, had a tremendous weight of expectation on her shoulders. She, like Mary Rand in 1960, was Britain's 'Golden Girl'. I wish we would learn not to build up these girls into gold medal certainties before they have even competed in the Olympics. Lillian will, I am sure, win a gold medal one day if only she goes on with her athletics. But I do hope that she realises that a close relative is not the best coach for any athlete—or perhaps it is her father who should realise this and hand over the care of Lillian's athletic career to those who really know what they are doing. There is so much more to winning an Olympic title than just running. There has to be what the French would term an 'ambiance' of calm and control and it was in this department that Lillian failed today. 'Failed' in this context is a stupid word—I should not use it. She won the silver medal in a new United Kingdom national record and that is an astounding performance for any girl of nineteen.

Amos Biwott won the steeplechase and I do not believe that he got a foot wet while doing so! I had expected Biwott to go out to the front, as he had done in his heat, and set a reasonably fast pace. After all, he and Kogo were the only two highlanders in the race, and one would think they would make the most of this advantage. But instead the field set off funereally and the first kilometre took 3 min 4.2 sec, with Kogo just in the lead from the Frenchman, Villain, who had run so well in his heat. With three laps to go the defending champion, Gaston Roelants, speeded up the pace and passed the 2000 metres mark in 6 min 3.2 sec—still incredibly slow for an Olympic final. With a lap and a quarter to go Roelants started to fade and Kogo took the lead. At the bell, Biwott was out of the race, some thirty yards back from a bunch of five runners—Kogo, George Young, the American who has had a vast amount of altitude training this year, Kerry O'Brien, Roelants, and the Russian, Morozov (the other Russian, Viktor Kudinski, the European champion, had dropped out just after the second water jump with an injury to his left leg).

In the back straight Young, who has not lost a race all season at any distance from a mile to a marathon, shot into the lead, with the young Australian just behind him, and Kogo, who because of the height must be the favourite, in third place. The medals seemed to be between these three. As I watched them go into the last water jump, I swung my binoculars back through the field and there, running twice as fast as anyone else—or so it seemed—was Biwott. He almost sprinted into the water jump, took another of his prodigious leaps, and gained about five yards. As they came into the finishing straight Kogo surged past Young and O'Brien, but behind him came Biwott and no one could stop him. He won by a clear five yards in 8 min 51.0 sec, with Kogo second in 8 min 51.6 sec, and George Young third in 8 min 51.8 sec.

I do not know quite what to make of it. Undoubtedly Biwott has tremendous ability, but I find it very strange that a man can win an Olympic title some four months after taking up the event. He cannot hurdle properly and he runs with a stride reminiscent of a woman chasing after a bus. Yet he could turn out to be the greatest steeplechaser we have ever seen, and maybe bring the world record down to a time in the region of 8 min 10 sec—which is where it ought to be. Of course, if he had run such a race at sea-level he would not have been in the first three, because you cannot give the world's best steeplechasers twenty or thirty yards in the last lap and still expect to win.

This strange day was made even stranger by the happenings in the 200 metres. In the semi-finals John Carlos and Tommie Smith both equalled the Olympic record of 20.1 sec and there was no doubt in anyone's mind that the gold medal lay between these two. But Tommie Smith appeared to be in trouble with a muscle. He was all right during the race, but he pulled up rather sharply and then limped off the track. There are reports that he has slightly pulled a muscle in his groin, but he has had it strapped up tightly and is going to run. 'The gold medal means a lot to me.'

When they came off the bend in the final, John Carlos was well in the lead, and then suddenly Smith changed gear, making the field look like second-raters. His long, lean body did not seem to be touching the ground as he came flying up the finishing straight to win by a clear two yards, despite the fact that he threw his arms into the air well before the tape. Carlos, well beaten, gave up just before the tape, and Peter Norman, the Australian, just snatched the silver medal from him.

Jim Hines has the title 'The fastest man in the world', but I believe that Smith is faster than Hines from a flying start. Those last eighty yards of his were as unbelievable as Bob Hayes's last eighty yards in the sprint relay in Tokyo. But, of course, the sensation was reserved for the victory ceremony. There had been many rumours that Smith and Carlos would make some sort of demonstration, and indeed they had worn calf-length black socks in both the heats and finals. When eventually, late in the evening, under the floodlights, they came out for the victory ceremony we could see that both of them had rolled their tracksuit trousers up to show the black socks. In one hand they wore a black leather glove, and in the other hand they carried a black Puma shoe.

As they stood on the victory rostrum they raised the gloved hand in the clenched fist salute of the Black Power Movement—and in the other hand they held the Puma shoe aloft. In one hand idealism and in the other hand commercialism. When the National Anthem was played they turned towards the flag, bowed their heads and raised their black-gloved, clenched fists.

At the press conference afterwards they said that they had demonstrated to show that black people are united. 'We are black, and proud to be black, and white America will only give us credit for being Olympic champions. But black America will understand.'

I must admit to some sympathy for their demonstration, because I believe that Tommie Smith is right when he said: 'If I do something good then I am an American, but if I do something bad then I am a Negro.' In their own country they are treated as first-class athletes but as second-class citizens. Many people think that they should not have dragged politics into an Olympic victory ceremony, but can human rights be classified as politics? In the next few days I found many athletes, both black and white, who were in sympathy with their stand for equal human rights. But I did not find a single athlete who was in sympathy with their commercial demonstration, for all the athletes in the village know that these two, like so many other leading athletes, have taken money from the shoe firms.

The only British competitors engaged today had rather mixed fortunes. Both Dick Steane and Ralph Banthorpe were knocked out in the semi-finals of the 200 metres, but as both recorded 20.8 sec, there is nothing to complain about. Alan Pascoe had rotten luck in the heats of the 110 metres hurdles. He equalled the United Kingdom record with a time of 13.9 sec. Yet he was only fourth. The first three in each heat and the fastest loser qualified for the final, and Alan missed being the fastest loser by no more than one hundredth of a second. Stuart Storey and Mike Parker both clocked 14.1 sec, their fastest times of the season, but it was not good enough.

In the first round of the 400 metres Colin Campbell and Martin Winbolt Lewis qualified for the second round (Winbolt Lewis running a personal best of 46.2 sec), but Howard Davies was knocked out. Both Derek Boosey and Fred Alsop, who has been troubled by injuries all season, failed to qualify in the triple jump. The Italian Giuseppe Gentil broke the eight-year-old world record with a hop, step and jump of 56 ft $1\frac{1}{4}$ in.

Our field events athletes are often criticised because of their meagre contribution to the points total of international matches, but this season we have seen some outstanding performances from some of them, and none more outstanding than today's hammer throw by thirty-seven-year-old Howard Payne. He knew that he would have to throw a personal best in order to qualify for the final, and he did it with a magnificent 223 ft 3 in., a personal improvement this year of over fourteen feet. It was, of course, a new United Kingdom record.

In the women's pentathlon the women's team captain Mary Peters improved her Tokyo performance by six points, but the standard has risen so much that she was placed ninth instead of fourth as in Tokyo. We have found a worthy successor to Mary Rand in the seventeen-year-old schoolgirl Sue Scott, who notched up 4786 points (a personal best) to come tenth. This girl has gold medal potential, but whisper it carefully, for we do not want her to be christened 'the Golden Girl of 1972'.

Finally, in the cool of the evening, after seven hours of pole vaulting, five men were still left in the competition when the bar was raised to 17 ft $8\frac{1}{2}$ in.—just half an inch below the world record. Three men, Bob Seagren of the United States, Claus Schiprowski of West Germany and Wolfgang Nordwig of East Germany, cleared this incredible height. But it was Seagren who won the gold medal because he had fewer failures at lower heights. So once again a United States athlete wins the pole vault to preserve the American monopoly in this event. But it was mighty close—Europe is catching up.

11
'OH GOD, IT'S OVER'

Thursday, October 17th

Damn the weather! Just when we needed a cool day it has turned sizzling hot.

This is the day when Paul Nihill, the twenty-nine-year-old bank manager's assistant from Thornton Heath, Surrey, is determined to change his 'failure' in Tokyo into success in Mexico City. I should say that it is Paul himself who used the word 'failure' about his Tokyo performance. But it was only his 'failure' to win a gold medal that rankles with him, for he was one of the successes of that great Tokyo team, winning the silver medal in the punishing fifty kilometres walk. In the past four weeks Paul has been striding all over Mexico City and showing the best form in his life. I have never seen anyone so determined to win a gold medal.

He set out this afternoon at 2.20, when the sun was scorching through my shirt and feeling as if it was burning my back. In front of him lay a course of thirty-one and a quarter miles and approximately four and a quarter hours of intense effort. At 3.30 I dashed outside the stadium to see him come past on one of the loops of this long course. The sun was searing off the concrete road, hurting my eyeballs.

Paul was the pace-setter and there were only three men who could keep with him—two Russians, Gennady Agapov and Sergey Grigorjev, plus the East German, Christoph Hohne. Paul was fresh enough to turn and ask Colin Campbell, the 400 metres runner, whether he had qualified for the semi-finals.

An hour later, when at last it was beginning to cool, Paul started to weave from side to side of the road. 'I thought,' he told me afterwards, 'that the crowd was barging into me and I said to myself: "I'll get annoyed in a minute." Then I saw the green line marking the route and tried to keep to that. Then I knew it was I who was doing the barging. I fell in the road and tried to get up. A woman said, "Are you all right?" and her words were echoing, echoing in my head. Then there was the siren. I was looking up at the roof of an ambulance. Everything was spinning and I thought, "Oh God, it's over!" I thought before the race I'd be the last man to come back in an ambulance. I thought of all the sacrifices, and my wife and my family and letting them all down, and I started to cry. They say that it's not manly to cry, but I cried. Then, bang, bang—the nurse was slapping my face. It didn't make any odds. I turned the other way and cried. Then the ambulance went into orbit.'

Paul's troubles were probably due to the heat more than the altitude. He had walked himself into a complete state of dehydration—the same trouble that affected Jim Peters in the last half-mile of the 1954 marathon at the Commonwealth Games in Vancouver. The first thing that starts to go is your balance, hence this weaving from side to side and barging into the crowd. Later, in the evening, Paul was well enough to toy with a meal in the Olympic village restaurant. He wanted to tell it all, to get it out of his system. But at midnight, the chef d'équipe of the dressage team found Paul walking round the village and was worried enough to call a doctor. Two hours later, Paul, still unable to sleep, was pouring out his story in a letter to his wife.

Can you really put into words what drives men like this? His was the most gallant performance of any member of the British team, and all he has to show for it is his own satisfaction that he bid for the gold medal and that it was a most courageous bid.

With Nihill out of the race, Christoph Hohne went on to win by the incredible margin of more than ten minutes. His time was 4 hr 20 min 13.6 sec, with Antal Kiss of Hungary second in 4 hr 30 min 17.0 sec and Larry Young of the United States third in 4 hr 31 min 55.4 sec. Bryan Eley, who describes himself as a cigar mechanic, was a very creditable seventh, beating the Mexican José Pedraza—the man who had won the silver medal in the twenty kilometres walk. Pedraza did his usual blinding finish in the stadium. I focused my binoculars on his feet to see whether he really was walking. Suddenly I saw a torrent of liquid fall on to the track and I looked up and saw that this incredible Mexican was being sick as he completed the last fifty yards.

They are tough, these walkers, but none tougher than Shaun Lightman, the third British competitor, who collapsed at the thirty-five kilometres mark but got back on to his feet to finish the course in eighteenth position. That evening Lightman, a twenty-five-year-old schoolmaster from Croydon, was slumped over a sink in the Olympic village, retching his guts out.

It was only eight years ago that the first black African, Abebe Bikila, won an Olympic gold medal and proved the potential of the African people, who were just emerging from the darkness of hunger and disease. On Sunday we had proof of their progress when all the medals in the 10,000 metres were won by African athletes. Today the pattern was repeated in the 5000 metres. But today the highland Africans were beaten by a lowlander—Mohamed Gammoudi, a twenty-nine-year-old sergeant-major in the Tunisian Army.

Gammoudi has spent long periods training at high altitude and he has competed here, in Mexico City, for the last three years in the pre-Olympic meets, winning both the 5000 and 10,000 metres in 1965 and in 1967. He has been given unlimited time off from the army and has spent much of it at the French high-altitude training centre at Font Romeu in the Pyrenees. Nevertheless, he was still at a disadvantage to those men born at altitude, which makes his victory today a gallant and very popular one.

The Kenyans were beaten by their own tactical mistake. Everyone expected them to make the pace as hard as possible, but instead it was Ron Clarke, who led the field of thirteen runners (Mamo Wolde was reserving himself for the marathon and the American, Batchelor, was another non-starter for some unknown reason) in a slow time of 2 min 53.5 sec for the first kilometre. Then Kipchoge Keino, the favourite for the event, went into the lead, but he hardly increased the pace and the 2000 metres mark was passed in 5 min 44.0 sec (2 min 50.5 sec for the kilometre). Inexplicably, Keino made no attempt to speed up the pace, and it was the Russian, Nickolay Sviridov, who led through the 3000 metres mark in 8 min 38.8 sec (the slowest kilometre so far—2 min 54.8 sec). Clarke went ahead again with five and a half laps still to go and passed the 4000 metre mark in 11 min 30.8 sec (the last kilometre in 2 min 52.0 sec). Compare these times with Clarke's world record in which he averaged 2 min 39.3 sec for each kilometre. This Olympic field is already 53.5 sec slower!

With three and a half laps to go, Clarke made his effort, but he just could not keep it up for long enough and it was Gammoudi who took the lead with two laps to go. Gammoudi led the field past the bell with Temu, the 10,000 metres winner, in second place and Keino looking very threatening in third place. Juan Martinez, the Mexican, was hanging on gamely to fourth place with Clarke a couple of yards behind.

Gammoudi slipped down the back straight with his smooth stride, but now his head was beginning to roll with fatigue and it looked a stone-cold certainty that Keino would be able to pass him in the finishing straight. But Gammoudi, who won a silver medal in Tokyo and a bronze medal here in Mexico, was not going to give up. From some depth of his small body he summoned up another effort and held the Kenyan off, all the way up the finishing straight. His winning time was 14 min 5.0 sec with Keino second in 14 min 5.2 sec, Temu third in 14 min 6.4 sec, Martinez fourth in 14 min 10.8 sec, and a very tired Ron Clarke fifth in 14 min 12.4 sec. The Ethiopian Wahib Masresha was sixth, so that four of the first six places went to highland athletes!

Clarke calls Gammoudi 'the best tactician in athletics' and it is a judgment that I would endorse. He ran a brilliant race today, and if Clarke was not to win, then there is no more popular victor amongst the athletes than Gammoudi, the most friendly, charming sergeant-major that I know.

Clarke, at the age of thirty-one, with family responsibilities and a new job to find when he gets back to Australia, was planning to retire after these Games. But in losing again today he must go on. 'Judgment of yourself,' he said to me that evening, 'comes from within you. Deep down I knew that in Tokyo there was a doubt about whether I had pushed myself to the limits. But here I know I did. I'm satisfied with myself.'

But he is not. This quest to prove himself a great champion, as well as the greatest of all distance runners, still pursues him. He now knows that he must go on until Edinburgh where the Commonwealth Games will be held in 1970. I asked him why and

I asked him also to explain this compulsion of an athlete that drives him on. He looked into the distance and said nothing for a minute. Then he said, 'I suppose Kipling said it. How does it go? Something like: "If you can dream and plan and build and see it all tumble down around you . . . and start again".'

Now that I am back in London I have been able to look up that verse of Kipling's, a most unfashionable but still great writer. It is worth repeating it in full, for it has much relevance to the situation.

> 'If you can dream—and not make dreams your master;
> If you can think—and not make thoughts your aim;
> If you can meet with triumph and disaster
> And treat those two impostors just the same;
> If you can bear to hear the truth you've spoken
> Twisted by knaves to make a trap for fools,
> Or watch the things you gave your life to, broken,
> And stoop and build them up with worn-out tools . . .'

Ron's body is not yet worn out and I know he has the courage to build his dreams up yet again.

Now for the British fortunes on this day—and they have been mixed as usual. In the women's 800 metres Sheila Taylor, with a time of 2 min 4.1 sec (a personal best), and Pat Lowe, with a time of 2 min 9.5 sec, qualified for the semi-finals. But Joan Page was last in her heat with a time of 2 min 10.2 sec. Both Colin Campbell and Martin Winbolt Lewis failed to survive the second round of the 400 metres, although Winbolt Lewis must be very pleased with a personal best time of 45.9 sec. In the women's 200 metres Maureen Tranter did not survive the first round in the morning, despite running her fastest time ever of 23.5 sec, and Lillian Board failed to survive the semi-finals in the afternoon even though she equalled her best time of 23.4 sec. Personal bests are just not good enough in this class of competitions.

None of our three girls, Ann Wilson, Pat Pryce and Pat Jones, survived the first round of the 80 metres hurdles. Pat Pryce had the misfortune to pull a muscle ten days ago and she pulled it again today over the second flight of hurdles. In the high jump Barbara Inkpen came thirteenth with a leap of 5 ft 6 in.—two and a half inches less than she cleared in the qualifying round yesterday. Howard Payne, too, could not quite produce his form of yesterday and was tenth in the final of the hammer with 221 ft 10 in.—his second best throw ever.

In the qualifying round of the long jump this morning Lynn Davies nearly gave his supporters a heart attack when he fouled on his first two attempts, but, great competitor that he is, came through on his last jump to qualify with 26 ft 0½ in. Perhaps this is not a bad sign because Lynn did exactly the same thing in the qualifying rounds at Tokyo, when, of course, he went on to win the gold medal.

I reserve until the end the most incredible final of the afternoon —the triple jump. This was an orgy of record breaking. The first seven men broke the Olympic record and the first five men broke the world record. Imagine your feelings when you break the world record and yet only come fifth! Viktor Saneyev of Russia was the gold medal winner with 57 ft 0¾ in.—fourteen and a quarter inches better than the old world record.

These incredible performances are due to a combination of the tartan track, the reduced air resistance, the intense competition and the world-wide improvement in standards—and how many inches are due to which of these factors is unknown. But it is worth recording that in 1955, when the Pan American Games were held in Mexico City, the great Brazilian triple-jumper, Da Silva, improved the world record by more than a foot. Is it any wonder that many people are saying that the International Amateur Athletic Federation should now inaugurate a new class of world records—those set at altitude!

12
'I CAN'T GO ON. WHAT IS THE POINT?'

Friday, October 18th

'Everybody has two legs, everybody can jump,' said Bob Beamon, a twenty-two-year-old, 6 ft 3 in., 11 st 6 lb, American university student. Maybe—but not everybody can jump like Bob Beamon.

Today he was ridiculous. Not only did he beat two world-record holders and the Olympic champion, but he stupefied them by taking off into orbit and leaping the prodigious distance of 29 ft 2½ in.

We are used to spectacular performances in the explosive events at this Games, but this jump is really out of this world. Let us go back more than thirty years and remember that in 1935 the incomparable Jessie Owens set a world long-jump record of 26 ft 8¼ in. That record lasted for twenty-nine years and then it was only beaten by one inch. In 1965, thirty years after Jessie Owens' leap, Ralph Boston, the 1960 Olympic champion, took the record up to 27 ft 5 in.—a distance that was equalled by the Russian Igor Ter-Ovanesyan here in Mexico City last year. Today Bob Beamon broke that record by one and threequarter feet. I have not got a superlative in my own vocabulary to describe such an improvement.

We always knew that Beamon had tremendous talent. Last week Lynn Davies said: 'If Beamon hits the take-off board right we can all forget it. He's got far more natural ability than anyone. Ralph [Boston] said to me: "Don't get him angry, Lynn, or he will jump right out of the pit".'

Luckily the Olympic pit was long enough but they will have to do some lengthening of most of the pits in the world if this man Beamon is going to go on competing. The shattering thing about his jump was that it was the very first legitimate jump of the competition. The three men who jumped before Beamon had all fouled when the tall Negro came onto the runway. He came down the tartan strip at a tremendous pace but had to chop his stride slightly to hit the take-off board. Then he soared into the air and I thought that he was imagining himself to be taking part in the high jump. I didn't see where he landed because his figure was obscured by an official. But it was obviously a good one, for the crowd were gasping with astonishment. The officials seemed to take an awfully long time to measure it, but then Beamon was coming back down the runway leaping into the air. He grabbed Ralph Boston and kissed him. Then he fell on the track and kissed the ground. 'I was thanking that man up there,' he said, 'for letting me hit the ground right here.'

Then on to the electronic scoreboard came the figures 8.90. In the press box we grabbed for our metric conversion tables. Someone said, 'That's 29 ft 2½ in.' Someone else said, 'Don't be bloody ridiculous.' But it was so. This incredible American Negro had left twenty-eight feet out of the record book.

Lynn Davies turned to Ralph Boston and said, 'I can't go on. What is the point?' Indeed the competition was over—without Ralph Boston, Igor Ter-Ovanesyan or Lynn Davies even jumping. During the second round it started to rain, and that further dampened their spirits. I should record that when the competition was all over a twenty-five-year-old blond German, Klaus Beer, had won the silver medal with a leap of 26 ft 10½ in. and that Ralph Boston had won the bronze medal with 26 ft 9¼ in. This is Ralph's last competition and I will be very sorry to see him retire, for there is no nicer man in athletics. He won a gold medal in Rome, a silver medal in Tokyo and a bronze medal here.

Lynn Davies has been criticised for giving up, but I have never heard more ridiculous criticism in my life. Those who make it, do not realise the competitive spirit this man has. He has won the gold medal at the Olympic Games, the Commonwealth Games and the European championships, and today nothing less than the gold medal would satisfy him. He was prepared to jump further than he has ever jumped before, but when Beamon shattered the bounds of possibility by jumping two feet further than Lynn has ever jumped before, there was nothing he could do but to accept the facts. That night he said to me: 'It is not real.' Instead of criticising him I admire him for his attitude: today it either had to be another gold medal or nothing. Lynn Davies only plays for big stakes.

The Americans, as expected, made a clean sweep in the 400 metres finals, but earlier today there was some doubt whether Lee Evans, the favourite, would compete at all. Last night the United States Olympic Committee sat in judgement on Tommie Smith and John Carlos. At four o'clock this morning they issued a statement saying that these two athletes had been suspended from the team and would have to leave the Olympic village. At one stage this morning Lee Evans said that he would withdraw from the 400 metres as a protest against this decision but then Carlos asked him to run.

It almost goes without saying that his winning time of 43.8 sec was a new world record. In the American Olympic trials at Lake Tahoe, Evans knocked half a second off Tommie Smith's world record, but on that occasion he was wearing the illegal 'brush' spikes. Today he was wearing 'legal' spikes, and so, in the space of two months, the world record has been lowered by the incredible margin of seven-tenths of a second—partly due to the tartan track and partly due to the reduced air resistance at altitude. Once again, as in the American Olympic trials, Larry James was only one-tenth of a second behind and Ron Freeman made it a clean sweep for the United States with third place in 44.4 sec.

On their way to the victory rostrum all three gave the clenched-fist salute and all three wore black berets. When asked at the press conference what was the significance of the berets, Lee Evans replied: 'We wore them because it was raining!'

He and his two compatriots brought the temperature down considerably by neatly dodging most of the political questions. But when asked whether he felt a responsibility to his Race when running, he said: 'I won this gold medal for black people in the United States and for black people all over the world.' Later another journalist asked him if he won his medal for anyone else. Evans replied: 'Yes, I did. I have a lot of white friends in San José [his university] and in Mexico and all over the world.'

When asked to explain the apparent superiority of the American Negro in all the short-distance events he said: 'There are a lot of different theories but my theory is that this may be our only outlet. I wouldn't have a scholarship to university if I wasn't a good runner. Maybe a white boy can get an education because his parents can pay for it, but I wouldn't be going to school right now if I hadn't got an athletic scholarship. That's my theory—others may have a different one.'

The tall Polish brunette, Irena Szewinska, better known by her maiden name of Kirszenstein, broke her own world record when winning the 200 metres in a time of 22.5 sec. But the sensation of this race was a seventeen-year-old blonde Australian Raelene Boyle, who came second with 22.7 sec, a new Commonwealth record. Raelene, one of the prettiest, if not the prettiest, girl in athletics, had come fourth in the 100 metres final and if there was ever a worthy successor to the great Australian sprinter Betty Cuthbert then it is this small girl. A lot can happen in four years but the betting now is that she will be the sprint star of Munich.

There are not many British athletes left by this stage of the games, but both John Whetton and John Boulter ran tactically mature races in the heats of the 1500 metres and qualified for tomorrow's semi-finals. But young Maurice Benn was nowhere near qualifying with eighth place in his heat in a time of 3 min 56.4 sec—equivalent to approximately 4 min 14 sec for the mile.

In the semi-finals of the women's 800 metres both Pat Lowe and Sheila Taylor qualified with ease. The prospects for tomorrow's final were turned upside down when the favourite Vera Nikolic, the twenty-year-old Jugoslavian girl, dropped out of the first semi-final after only 300 metres. There appeared to be nothing wrong with her. When she had recovered her breath she trotted up the straight, avoided the finishing tape which was waiting for her fellow competitors to complete the race, picked up her shoes and burst into tears.

Slowly she made her way out of the stadium, not turning to look at the finish of the race. Outside, she went to the bridge which spans the road and leaned over it, 'tearing her hair', as one witness put it. An official hauled her back and she fell screaming to the ground.

Her coach is to blame and he should never be allowed near

another athlete. He has had this young Jugoslavian girl, who holds the world record for the 800 metres, out on the training track three times a day for the past three weeks, working her so hard, and reducing her to tears, that even the Australian distance runners, hard trainers themselves, wonder how anyone's body, much less the body of a woman, can stand it.

13
'PLEASE STAND BY ME IN MY HOUR OF NEED'

Saturday, October 19th

'I was frightened to go with them. I'm a coward because I had a lot left at the finish.' So said Sheila Taylor after coming fourth in the 800 metres today and her words only prove that an athlete is his own, or her own, most vehement critic. I would hardly call it cowardice to come fourth in an Olympic final; in a personal best time; in your first international season.

In the absence of the world-record holder Vera Nikolic the race was very open, with an outside chance that the small, blonde schoolteacher, Pat Lowe, from Birmingham, who has been running extremely well in training, could repeat Ann Packer's (now Mrs. Brightwell) exploit in Tokyo.

Sheila Taylor, a civil servant from Coventry, ran a very inexperienced race, but Pat Lowe ran with perfect judgment, always being with the leaders and staying with the tall American black girl, Madeline Manning, when she made her break down the back straight. But as they came round the final bend one could see that Pat was in trouble while the American girl strode away to an easy victory in the new Olympic record of 2 min 0.9 sec.

This also beats the listed world record held by Ann Packer, but there is a time of 2 min 0.5 sec awaiting ratification, set up by Vera Nikolic at the Crystal Palace in London earlier this year.

As Pat Lowe faded in the straight ('I died over the last forty yards'), she was overtaken by Ilona Silai of Rumania, who won the silver medal with a time of 2 min 2.5 sec, and Maria Gommers of Holland, who took the bronze with 2 min 2.6 sec. Sheila Taylor came through very fast in the last fifty metres to take fourth place in 2 min 3.8 sec, with Pat Lowe hanging on grimly for sixth place in 2 min 4.2 sec.

I am sure that Sheila will learn that in the Olympic Games the medals go to those athletes who are prepared to risk all. But one cannot blame her for her tactics today because she is only twenty-two and this is her first year of international competition. In fact, she was a late choice for the team after Anne Smith had failed to recover from an injury.

I am absolutely convinced that if Lillian Board had run in the 800 metres today, instead of the 200 metres, as her second event she could have taken the gold or silver medal. But unfortunately Lillian will not attain her true stature as an athlete until she is coached professionally instead of by her father. Family relationships do not work in sport, although after Vera Nikolic's experiences with a professional coach one can understand a father's reluctance to hand his daughter over. Today Miss Nikolic, on the verge of a nervous breakdown, has been flown home to Belgrade. She has sent a cable to her mother saying, 'Please stand by me in my hour of need.' Sport should never become as important as this in one's life, but then the whole of Vera's life is geared to sport—including her government flat in Belgrade. At one moment she is saying that she never wants to see a track again and in the next moment she is saying that she will come back and show the world. If she does, I hope she gets herself a new coach.

It was a long day in the stadium from ten in the morning under a blazing sun to six in the evening with the sky looking as if Armageddon was approaching—a pleasant, gentle day with the jungle tom-toms beating whenever an African or West Indian team managed to reach tomorrow's finals of the relays. At times it sounded as if we were inside a giant's stomach—a giant with a bad attack of Montezuma's revenge.

Two out of the three British relay teams are through to the final and the third team—the men's 4×100 metres relay—have put in a protest against the result of their semi-final.

Barrie Kelly, taking over the baton on the last leg from Ralph Banthorpe, suddenly found the incoming Polish runner staggering with flaying arms into his lane. 'He was like a kite. I had to run round him.' The Poles were placed fourth, thus qualifying for the final tomorrow, whereas the British team were fifth in 39.4 sec.

The jury will see a videotape of the race later this evening. I think there is no doubt that Kelly was hindered only fractionally and one must remember that the Pole who staggered into his lane had already handed the baton over with the Polish anchor man already well on his way.

Whatever the result of the appeal, the British team have no chance of a medal tomorrow, although they naturally want to have another crack at the British record in these perfect sprinting conditions. With really good baton changing they could get below 39.0 sec—not that that means much in these artificial conditions. If one really wants to set up a British sprint record the crater of Kilimanjaro might be the place to go!

Earlier in the afternoon the British girls—Anita Neal, Maureen Tranter, Janet Simpson and Lillian Board—came third in their semi-final with a time of 43.9 sec, which breaks the British record set up four years ago in Tokyo by a tenth of a second. In the 4 × 400 metres relay the British team of Martin Winbolt Lewis, Colin Campbell, Dave Hemery and John Sherwood qualified for the final with a thoroughly competent run in 3 min 3.6 sec.

In the 1500 metres semi-finals John Whetton found himself up against Jim Ryun and Kipchoge Keino. I wonder how anybody could seed those two, co-favourites for the title, in the same semi-final. It was an extremely slowly run race, the first lap taking 68 sec and the 800 metres taking 2 min 12.7 sec—times that would look very ordinary in the British schoolboys championships.

With 600 metres to go, Keino started to stir things up, but on the back straight of the final lap the field were still all bunched tightly together. Then Whetton started to show his speed, but he had hardly accelerated when Ryun came storming past with one of those bursts which have made him the world-record holder. His time of 3 min 51.2 sec (Keino was second in 3 min 51.4 sec and Whetton third in 3 min 52.0 sec) is equivalent to a mile in just under 4 min 10 sec—very slow running for an Olympic semi-final.

Fear of the altitude seems to have got into the 1500 metres runners because the other semi-final was run at an equally funereal pace—67.6 sec for the first lap, 2 min 14.9 sec for 800 metres, and 3 min 14.6 sec for three laps. It is the sort of pace that should suit John Boulter, one of Europe's top half-milers. But he seemed to run into a brick wall in the finishing straight and never had a chance of getting into the final. Bodo Tummler, of West Germany, who won the 1500 metres in the 'Little Olympics' last year, ran the last lap in 52.2 sec to win this semi-final.

Today has mainly been a clearance day before the climax tomorrow. What a day it will be: the battle between Ryun and Keino in the 1500 metres with Bodo Tummler and John Whetton, a real outsider but a very determined one, waiting to pounce if either of the stars makes the slightest mistake; the relays, always the most thrilling of athletic events; and finally the centrepiece of the athletic programme—the arrival of the iron men who have run 26 miles 385 yards under the Mexican sun, through streets with little shade, in an atmosphere which leaves the lungs gasping for precious, rare oxygen.

14
THE FOSBURY FLOP. 'IT'S MEDITATION'

Sunday, October 20th

I am very much afraid that this afternoon's activities may produce a crop of injured backs and broken necks around the world. The 'Fosbury Flop' brought its inventor and sole practitioner a gold medal today, and it has overshadowed even the 1500 metres and the marathon. Dick Fosbury breaks all the rules of high-jumping and yet he jumped 7 ft $4\frac{1}{2}$ in., a new Olympic record, this afternoon. No words can really describe his incredible technique. In fact, it is very difficult to analyse it even when watching it in person. The only way to understand this incredible technique is to watch a slow-motion film.

First of all there is the build-up, and that takes at least two or three minutes. Dick Fosbury, a big man—6 ft 4 in. and 13 st 1 lb—stands on the high-jump fan with his elbows tucked tightly into his sides and opens and closes his fists, and even when you are a hundred yards away you can see him willing himself over that bar. He says: 'I just kind of get the idea of falling over that bar. It's meditation.'

On his right foot he wears a white shoe and on his left foot a blue shoe, and he stands there rocking backwards and forwards, clenching and unclenching his fists for a good two minutes before he bounds forwards with four or five kangaroo-like strides, and then, as he takes off, he twists in a clockwise direction and dives backwards, over the bar. At the highest point of his trajectory he is looking upwards into the sky and then he falls, landing on the base of his neck and the top of his spine. It would have been a suicidal technique before the introduction of the new soft-landing pits. The trouble is that there are going to be a lot of schoolboys who, having seen him on television, will want to imitate his style and they will be landing on sand, which is likely to produce a crop of injuries. Fosbury is saved by the new Port-a-pit, but this is a very expensive item of equipment. A Port-a-pit for the pole vault can cost as much as £1000, and although the landing area for the high jump is much smaller, it still costs enough to put it out of the reach of most schools.

Fosbury's style must be the despair of all athletic coaches, but I welcome it because it proves that the most important things in athletics are dedication, concentration, and the will to 'have a go'. These days some events have become completely tied up with technique. Erudite men will talk about the centre of gravity and moments of leverage, explaining with complicated diagrams the way to accomplish some feat with the maximum amount of mechanical efficiency. Then along comes this university student from Oregon and proves that all you have to do to win an Olympic title is jump higher than anybody else using a style that suits you!

I like Eddy Ottoz's remark. The Italian hurdler said: 'Athletics has got to the stage where if a man high-jumped holding a glass of whisky with an ice cube in it somebody would analyse the size, density and weight of the ice cube and prove that this was vital. Fosbury has proved that the only vital thing is to jump high.'

But let us get back to conventional athletics. Once in a decade there occurs a clash of supermen in the 'blue riband' event—the mile or its metric equivalent, the 1500 metres. In the early 1950s it was Roger Bannister versus John Landy—at that time the only two men who had broken four minutes for the mile. Eight years later we savoured the prospect of Herb Elliott versus Peter Snell. And that, to my mind, would have been the greatest clash of all, but we never did see it because of Herb's retirement.

Here we had an almost equally thrilling prospect to savour—Jim Ryun versus Kipchoge Keino. There is no doubt in my mind that at sea-level Ryun would have won. After all, he is the world-record holder at 3 min 51.1 sec for the mile—two seconds faster than Keino has ever run. And Ryan is also the world-record holder for the 1500 metres, with a time of 3 min 33.1 sec—exactly 3.6 sec faster than Keino has ever run.

But at 7000 ft the positions are reversed. Keino, who has spent all his life above the 6000 ft contour, has recently run an incredible 3 min 39.9 sec for the 1500 metres and he did it at a height of nearly 8000 ft at Thompson's Falls in Kenya. Ryun's best time at altitude is 3 min 43.0 sec. The odds, here in Mexico City, were weighted therefore in favour of Kipchoge Keino—but only if he ran a sensible race, and we have already seen that the Kenyans' tactics were very immature in both the 5000 metres and the 3000 metres steeplechase. If Keino was to win, then he, or his compatriot Jipcho, had to go out and make the pace really fast. If they dawdled, as they had done in the semi-finals, then Ryun's electric finish would give him the advantage.

Ten yards after the gun we knew that the Kenyans were not going to take any chances. Jipcho leapt into the lead, streaking round the first lap in 56.0 sec with the West German, Harald Norpoth, vainly trying to keep in touch. Keino was in third place and Ryun was trailing at the back of the field—indeed at one stage in the lap he was last. After 500 metres, with two laps still to go, Keino took over, determined that the pace should not slacken. At 800 metres, passed in 1 min 55.3 sec (a lap of 59.3 sec), Keino had eight yards on Bodo Tummler, Norpoth and John Whetton, who was running a superbly judged tactical race. Ryun was looking heavy and cumbersome, and was already twenty-five to thirty yards down. Unless Keino blew up in the last furlong, then Ryun had no chance at all.

One must pay tribute to Keino's courage. He knew what he had to do and he did it magnificently. Instead of taking the conventional rest in the third lap, he piled on the pace and passed the 1200 metres mark in 2 min 53.4 sec (the third lap had taken 58.1 sec). Now there was only 300 metres to go and Keino had twenty yards over Tummler, Norpoth and Whetton, who was still hanging grimly on. At last Ryun began to make up ground, and on the back straight he swept past Whetton and took the two Germans on the final bend. But there was never any chance that he would catch the incredible Keino.

Keino's time was 3 min 34.9 sec—beating Herb Elliott's Olympic record by 0.7 sec. Ryun was second in 3 min 37.8 sec—4.7 sec, or more than thirty yards, slower than his own world record. I believe that today we saw the equivalent of the first mile in under 3 min 50 sec. On the conventional conversion, Keino's time is the equivalent of about 3 min 53.0 sec for a mile, but if you estimate that the altitude slowed Ryun by about one second a lap, then I reckon Keino's performance equal to about 3 min 49.0 sec.

Many people criticised Ryun's tactics. They thought he should have kept closer to Keino, as Tummler, Norpoth and Whetton had done. But Ryun told me afterwards: 'If I'd gone through the 1200 metres mark in 2 min 53 sec I would have had a lot of trouble in finishing at all. I would have certainly thrown away any chance of a medal. I know this because I've tried it at altitude and I know that Keino set a pace that would have been suicide for me. There's so much talk about altitude, but few people really realise what it does to an athlete.' We chatted on about one or two things, principally about whether he felt that he would now have to keep on until Munich, and then, as he turned to leave, he said: 'I'll tell you one thing. These are "the Unfair Games".'

Nobody can begrudge Keino his success. He has not been at his best all season and he is reported to be suffering from gallstones. Furthermore, he was tied up in a traffic jam on his way to the stadium and had to jog the last mile—hardly a good preparation for an Olympic final! I do hope that somebody can assemble this field together again for a race at sea-level. With Jipcho to do some of the pace-making, I am sure we should see a new world record for the mile.

Immediately after the finish of the 1500 metres, I left the stadium, and drove into the city in an attempt to pick up the marathon runners. By a stroke of luck I met them at a crucial stage of the race. They were just turning into Chapultepec Park, having completed fifteen miles, with eleven miles 385 yards still to go. Naftali Temu had just made his break and was ten yards up on Tim Johnston and Mamo Wolde. Abebe Bikila was nowhere to be seen, and the fastest man in the world over this distance, Derek Clayton, the Lancashire-born Australian, was 100 yards back in ninth position.

Both Clayton and Bikila were running under severe handicaps. Clayton's training—an average of 163 miles a week for the past six months—has produced one permanent injury. He has a cyst under a knee cartilage which causes him acute pain, and he has a date with the surgeon as soon as he gets back to Australia. Bikila has a hairline fracture of a bone in his foot and has spent much of the last four days in bed.

Three miles further on Wolde has closed up with Temu and Johnston is nowhere in sight. Eventually, when he does appear, some 200 yards behind the two leaders, it is obvious that he is suffering from severe stomach cramp.

The Kenyan and the Ethiopian ran together for another two kilometres and then at the thirty-kilometres mark (nearly nineteen miles) Wolde started, as he explained afterwards: 'My good running'—and it certainly was good. Down the long Avenue Insurgentes he pulled away from the field to win by over three minutes from Kimihara of Japan and Mike Ryan of New Zealand. At the finish I could detect no sign of any sweat on Wolde. Even if Tim Johnston had been at his best I do not believe that he could have beaten the Ethiopian today.

Wolde's winning time of 2 hr 20 min 26.4 sec is not as fast as many people expected. The theory is that the altitude does not affect marathon runners as much as it does the 5000 and the 10,000 metres runners because it is stamina rather than lung capacity which counts in a marathon. So many people were prophesying a time of about 2 hr 15 min (as against Clayton's world best of 2 hr 9 min 36.4 sec). But undoubtedly the altitude has more effect than people thought. Heat also played a part, because the race was started at the stupid hour of three o'clock in the afternoon. It is time that the International Amateur Athletic Federation paid more attention to the needs of the athletes than the neat scheduling of the programme.

Bill Adcocks was the best of the British trio, finishing fifth in 2 hr 25 min 33.0 sec, with Tim Johnston eighth in 2 hr 28 min 4.0 sec. Jim Alder had a terrible time and, like Paul Nihill in the fifty kilometres walk, suffered from dehydration. He was extremely nervous before the start and was so knotted up in his stomach that he had to urinate four or five times in the hour before the start, and then again while actually on the starting line in the impressive Constitution Square. It was no wonder that he became dehydrated at about the thirty kilometres mark and lost his sense of balance.

Johnston, who has devoted a year of his life to training at altitude, made a small but fatal mistake—largely due to inexperience. He did not eat enough that morning. An hour before the race, when he was already at the start, he was desperately searching for something to fill the void in his stomach. For the first ten miles he felt a slight uneasiness, but he was running well within himself and enjoying the race. But then when Temu, followed by Wolde, started their break and Tim tried to follow he was suddenly gripped with the most terrible stomach cramp.

Back at the stadium, the United States team won the 4 × 100 metres relay, as expected, although they only had a yard over the Cuban team. The American baton-changing was not very impressive and it was Enrique Figuerola who came away from the last takeover with a clear yard over Jim Hines. But there was never any real doubt that Hines would catch him, and eventually he won by more than a yard. Inevitably, the United States team broke the world record—their time of 38.2 sec was a 0.4 sec improvement.

The world record was also broken by the United States girls in winning their sprint relay—their time of 42.8 sec was a massive 1.1 sec improvement. The British girls were seventh out of eight teams, but it is no disgrace to have run 43.7 sec for a new United Kingdom record—incidentally, 0.2 sec inside the old world record.

Finally, the United States made a clean sweep of the relay events by winning the 4 × 400 metres relay and it almost goes without saying that this, too, was in a new world record. They won by thirty yards in a time of 2 min 56.1 sec, which is an incredible average of 44.0 sec per man.

One always expects world records to be broken in relay events at the Olympic Games because it is only in an Olympic year that national teams get together for long periods. But it might be worth examining the tally of world records in other events and comparing it with the number broken in Tokyo. Excluding the relays, the only world records broken or equalled in Tokyo by the men were the 100 metres and the 400 metres. In Tokyo the women broke or equalled four world records—the 100 metres, 800 metres, long jump and javelin. Here in Mexico the men equalled or broke seven world records (again I am excluding the relays)—the 100 metres, 200 metres, 400 metres, 800 metres,

400 metres hurdles, long jump and triple jump. And the women's tally was exactly the same as in Tokyo—four records in 100 metres, 200 metres, long jump and shot.

Analysing the British team's performance, one finds, surprisingly, that they have won the smallest number of medals in any Olympics this side of the war. In 1948 at Wembley the team won seven medals; in 1952 in Helsinki they won five; in 1956 in Melbourne seven; in 1960 in Rome eight medals; in 1964 in Tokyo twelve medals including four gold. Here in Mexico City the tally was one gold (Dave Hemery), two silver (Sheila Sherwood and Lillian Board) and one bronze (John Sherwood). But I do not think we should be too depressed about these results. In all previous Olympics since the war a good proportion of our medals have come from the middle- and long-distance events—indeed in 1960 and in 1956 the only gold medals were in these events. Here at this altitude the team had no chance whatsoever of winning medals in any event over the 800 metres.

There is another trend, however, that we should notice. I feel that the British teams are likely to come home with fewer and fewer medals as time goes on. This is not because our standard is going down but because more and more people in the world are now achieving a standard of living which enables them to spend part of their daily life in recreation. We have seen the way Africa has emerged as a potent athletic force since 1960. But as yet we have seen no signs of the Asians proving their athletic potential. It will come one day. And when it does we shall look back on the four medals that we won in Mexico as a real bonanza.

15
'DAMN THE JURY. WE'LL SHOW THEM NOW'

Acapulco. Monday and Tuesday, October 21st and 22nd

Supercalifragilisticexpialidocious, commonly known as *Superdocious*, is a highly sophisticated 20-foot sailing dinghy belonging to the Flying Dutchmen class. Sailed by two blond young Englishmen with the names of Rod Pattisson and Iain Macdonald-Smith, *Superdocious* has shown as much superiority over its rivals down here in Acapulco as Dave Hemery did in the Olympic Stadium.

A week ago they won the first race in this Olympic regatta, but were then disqualified for 'taking the water' of the Canadian boat at the start of the race. They and their team manager, Vernon Stratton, disputed the jury's verdict and indeed have photographic evidence to prove that there was no justification for the disqualification. However, the jury refused to change their minds and this left Rod, Iain and *Superdocious* in a very exposed position. The Olympic Regatta consists of seven races of which six are counted. So now Rod, Iain and *Superdocious* had to make every one of the next six races count—they could not afford one bad race. Taking no chances, they proceeded to win them, one by one, until today, Monday, the last race of the regatta. Today they can play safe, for their points lead is so great that if their nearest rival, the West German boat, comes first then they must come no lower than twenty-fifth.

Determined not to be disqualified today, Rod and Iain started well away from the rest of the fleet. Despite this handicap, they sailed up through the fleet to come second to the Brazilian boat—the only time that *Superdocious* has been beaten here in Acapulco.

Rod and Iain were expected to win the gold medal—in fact they were the nearest thing to a certainty in the British team. But that is not always a comfortable position to be in, and they have had to keep their heads and forget that first painful disqualification.

Britain has a tremendous record in the Flying Dutchman class. You may remember that in the 1964 Olympics Keith Musto and Tony Morgan won the silver medal. The next year Dick Pitcher and Ian McCormick won the world championships in Italy. Two years later John Oakeley and David Hunt, in *Shadow*, again won the world championships in Montreal, and this year Rod Pattisson, Iain Macdonald-Smith and *Superdocious* won the European championships in Hungary and then beat Oakeley/Hunt and Musto/Morgan in the British trials. So, just like the American sprinters, Rod and Iain have had to emerge from a pyramid of talent that no other nation could match.

Rod Pattisson is twenty-five years old, 5 ft 9 in. high, $10\frac{1}{2}$ st, and a lieutenant in the Royal Navy. He is blond and sensible, and there is nobody in the 270-strong British Olympic team who has worked harder for his place or who has gone to such infinite trouble to make certain that everything possible has been done to turn that favouritism into reality.

He lives in Poole in a solid, prosperous house, given over entirely to the pursuit of 'messing about in boats'. His father was a Fleet Air Arm pilot and now works in London, organising exhibitions. He has two sisters, both married to keen dinghy helmsmen, and a younger brother, John, who was British Firefly champion in 1966.

He himself started sailing in a Cadet (that phenomenally successful Jack Holt design) which his father built, and at the age of seventeen he won the Cadet championships. He is very much a product of the dinghy-sailing boom which produces such fierce competition every weekend on every conceivable stretch of water in Britain.

While still at Dartmouth, Rod bought a very old Flying Dutchman for £220 which had absolutely everything wrong with it. He then proceeded to work through every part, changing and experimenting, until he had it going so well that he was able to notch up one victory over Oakeley and Hunt in their seemingly unbeatable *Shadow*. He says: 'The last thing you want to do is to buy a fast boat.' Having learnt every trick of tuning a Flying Dutchman, he invested £350 on a new boat built by Bob Hoare, of Christchurch, Hampshire, currently acknowledged to be the best builder of the class in the world.

It was delivered as a bare hull at Easter, 1966, when Rod was stationed on H.M.S. *Wakeful*, a frigate based on Portsmouth. For the next year he spent every conceivable moment of his spare time varnishing, painting and fitting out *Superdocious* (the name comes from a song in *Mary Poppins*) and then advertised in a yachting magazine for a crew: 'Ultimate aim Mexico 1968. Athletic, helmsman, 6 ft 5 in., $14\frac{1}{2}$ st.'

From the replies he chose a student at London University, Mike Young, and in their first regatta in March 1967 they came third to Oakeley/Hunt and Musto/Morgan. It was a good start to his Olympic campaign, but he knew that if he was to come out on top of the incredibly powerful British opposition he would have to concentrate on getting the maximum amount of international competition and on tuning the boat in between regattas.

The first objective was the San Remo-Monaco fortnight, but he had no crew—Mike Young was tied up with exams. Rod was away at sea on a submarine, H.M.S. *Opportune,* so his brother John (who at 5 ft 8 in. and $10\frac{1}{2}$ st is too short and light for the job) searched for a crew. He found Iain Macdonald-Smith, twenty-three years old, 6 ft 3 in. tall, 12 st 10 lb, and a good helmsman—a member of the Cambridge University team.

Together Rod and Iain came third at Monaco and second in the 1967 British championships. This was the most vital result of their career together, for it produced an invitation to the Flying Dutchman Open Week in Montreal, held in conjunction with the world championships, and to the 'Little Olympics' at Acapulco last October.

For a long time Rod felt guilty about the change of crew, but his allegiance had to be to Iain, with whom he had won that vital second place in the British championships. Besides, they were working so well together. 'It is a tremendous advantage,' says Rod, 'to have a good helmsman as crew. You think together. He understands and knows all your problems. We sail round a course as if we were both helming. I'm always talking aloud about what I'm doing and why, and Iain can add his opinion and we get the advantage of two helmsmen!'

But still they had the problem of defeating world champions Oakeley and Hunt if they were to compete in the Olympics. They tuned and tuned. 'Forty per cent of the battle,' says Iain, 'is boat speed. It is just like tuning a racing car.'

Their secret weapon for 1968 was a mast. They borrowed the idea from Helmar Pedersen, the Dane who emigrated to New Zealand and won the gold medal at Tokyo. Pedersen appeared last year with a new and very thin Australian mast. Rod liked the look of it and commissioned a fellow submariner to sit on the manufacturer's doorstep in Sydney until one was shipped to Britain. When it arrived they put all the cordage inside the groove which was only designed to take the bolt rope of the sail. It barely fitted, but it did give them a completely clean mast which was half an inch in diameter less than anyone else's. By such minutiae are titles—especially Olympic titles—won. With this mast Rod and Iain won the British trials—a harder job, they say now, than winning the gold medal.

Both Rod and Iain are very keen on a refined form of gamesmanship or 'out-psyching your opponent'. Any new piece of equipment—whether it works or not—immediately gives you a psychological advantage over your opponents and Rod and Iain have been producing new pieces of equipment here in Acapulco like magicians producing a rabbit from a hat.

I asked John Oakeley, who is here in Acapulco as a reserve, to explain to me how it was that Rod and Iain had shown so much superiority over the other crews. 'If there was some rule that made you go faster than the others,' said Oakeley, 'then there would be no interest in yachting. It's really a painstaking attention to details. You've got to have a boat of minimum weight with a very good finish. And then you must have a good mast and a good boom, good sails and a good rudder and good centreboard. Having got a fast boat you must then point it in the right direction!'

The attention to detail is even extended to their food. It was the British reserves—John Oakeley and David Hunt—who discovered that you could not think straight if you were half starved.

So they approached Professor de Jong at Horlicks and he made them up packs of concentrated, light-weight (vitally important) food that kept Oakeley and Hunt, during last year's world championships, and Pattisson and Macdonald-Smith here in Mexico, at peak efficiency. It is no coincidence that well prepared teams like the yachtsmen—and the equestrian team, who we hear today have won a gold medal in the three-day event—have done so well. They have approached the Olympics in a professional way—and the right sort of professionalism which in this context means a deep knowledge of your event plus the intelligence, time and persistence to apply that knowledge to every aspect.

I confess to a sense of pride in the way this yachting team have gone about their business. Vernon Stratton, the team manager, and his wife, the assistant team manager, have made certain that everything possible has been done for the competitors. They have brought their own meteorological expert—David Houghton from Bracknell—with them, and he has been able to give the British competitors some extremely accurate information based on the work he has been doing in the three weeks before the Games. With a horde of willing helpers he has also been able to measure the tides and to discover a strange phenomenon called 'The Slippery Sea'. This is a current created when the warm water on the surface of the ocean slides over the cooler sea below.

Rod and Iain now feel that their disqualification on the first day may not have done them so much harm as they thought at the time. 'It made all the other competitors feel sorry for us. Our attitude was "Damn that jury. We'll show them now." It certainly toughened up our mental attitude.'

The Flying Dutchman gold medal was not the only medal won by the British team. Robin Aisher, Paul Anderson and Adrian Jardine won the bronze medal in the 5.5 metres class and they only did it by a distance of two feet in the last race.

On Monday night, the whole team went out for a mammoth party and Rod Pattisson went to sleep for an hour in the middle of a cacophonous discotheque. He says that because of his submarine training he can sleep anywhere, but this is plain ridiculous.

16
'CONCENTRATION IS THE QUALITY THAT MAKES CHAMPIONS'

*Wednesday, Thursday and Friday,
October 23rd, 24th and 25th*

Back from Acapulco with a lot of events to catch up with. First, let us go back to last Saturday and that esoteric event, clay-pigeon shooting. Bob Braithwaite, a forty-three-year-old veterinary surgeon from Preston in Lancashire, won the gold medal with an astounding series of 187 successive 'pigeons'. These 'pigeons' are nothing more than a clay disc which are propelled out of a trap at anything up to 100 miles an hour. The shooter knows when one is going to appear because he gives the command for release, but he does not know which trap it will be released from—there are three traps for every shooting position—so he does not know whether the 'pigeon' will be flying from left to right, from right to left, or in a rising trajectory away from him.

The Olympic competition consists of 200 'pigeons' and Braithwaite started badly by missing the fifth because of the difficult early-morning light. 'I've never known light vary as much as it does here,' he said afterwards. Then he missed the thirteenth—'Sheer incompetence. I didn't see the bastard come out.' But after that Braithwaite did not miss a single 'pigeon'—187 successful shots for a total of 198, which equals the Olympic and world record set by Signor Mattarelli of Italy during the 1964 Olympic Games in Tokyo. Such a performance could only be accomplished by a man with no nerves at all. Braithwaite has no nerves—'At least I am not aware of any.'

There are only about 150 people practising this sport in England, and only three or four in world class. And this is not very surprising when you consider the cost. Braithwaite uses a Belgian gun which cost £560 and Belgian cartridges which cost £7 10s. per hundred. If you consider that you may use as many as 300 cartridges per competition (you are allowed to use both barrels at any one 'pigeon') it is not surprising that Braithwaite says: 'If you counted the cost you would stop shooting.'

When he was a boy Braithwaite shot anything that moved. Now he much prefers the inanimate clay pigeons. 'Concentration,' he says, 'is the quality that makes champions in shooting. I don't eat anything all day during a competition because I find food slows up my reflexes. So on the day of the competition I had nothing from seven o'clock in the morning until eight at night—thirteen hours on tea and coffee. You've got to be a bit of a nut to practise this game.'

The following day, Sunday, the three-day event team—Major Derek Allhusen, Staff-Sergeant Ben Jones, Richard Meade and the twenty-year-old nurse Jane Bullen—laid the basis for the gold medal which they won the following day. The cross-country and steeplechase course was naturally a very tough one and the day started very hot with holding and uneven going. This affected Jane Bullen on Our Nobby because she fell twice when Our Nobby went up to his hocks in mud. Then, in the middle of the day, just before Sergeant Ben Jones started, it began to rain—tropical rain. The river running through the course overflowed and at least two of the fences were under water. Ben Jones told me that the rain was like a sheet in front of him: 'I couldn't see the fences, just something dark looming up ahead. It was quite an experience. I wouldn't have missed it for anything, but I don't want to ride it again.'

The British team emerged from the downpour with almost fifty points' lead over the American team and more than 100 points over the Russian team. This meant that on the Monday they could knock down four fences in the show-jumping and still come first even if all the American riders had a clear round. In the event Major Allhusen and Ben Jones had clear rounds, with Richard Meade knocking down two fences. So the British team won with minus 175.93 points as against the United States' team with minus 245.87 points and the Australians with minus 331.26 points. Derek Allhusen won the individual silver medal.

Wednesday produced two silver medals and one bronze medal for the British team. In the first round of the show-jumping only two competitors had clear rounds—Bill Steinkraus of the United States on Snowbound and Marion Coakes, the pretty, blue-eyed blonde girl from Hampshire, on her incredible pony Stroller. Stroller is the only pony to have ever competed in the Olympic show-jumping events. He is only 14.2 hands high, which is at least two hands (about eight inches) smaller than most of his rivals. 'He's a freak, really,' says Marion. What a freak!

Despite suffering from a sore tooth, Stroller jumped clear round the course, which Bill Steinkraus himself says '. . . is not quite legitimate show-jumping. When they left just six obstacles in for the second round and raised them it really became a puissance course, and not really fair as an Olympic course.' Perhaps it was just a little too big for Stroller, because in the second round he hit two fences for eight faults, whereas Steinkraus and Snowbound only hit one. David Broome, with four faults in the first round and eight faults in the second round, won the bronze medal riding Mr. Softee. It is his second bronze, for he also came third in the Rome Olympics in 1960 on Sunsalve.

Marion was once offered 100,000 dollars (over £40,000) for Stroller by an American. 'I couldn't sleep for a week thinking about the money,' she says, 'but I didn't have another good horse, so I didn't sell him.' He is now sixteen years old and should have another two years of show-jumping in him. Marion is only twenty-one and should have many more years at the top of the tree.

Down at the swimming pool, eighteen-year-old Martyn Woodroffe, a schoolboy from Cardiff, proved that a British swimmer, with some dedicated training and some guts in competition, can win an Olympic medal. I was able to make only one visit to the Olympic pool and I had the luck to walk in just as the men's 200 metres butterfly event started. Martyn Woodroffe was in lane one, nearest to the press stand, and at the half-distance we were all shattered to see him well up with the leader, Carl Robie of the United States, and ahead of the boy prodigy Mark Spitz. As Martyn went down the pool again towards his last turn, I thought that he was fractionally ahead. But then, on the way back, Robie splashed his way to the front to win the gold medal in 2 min

8.7 sec, with Woodroffe second in 2 min 9.0 sec and John Ferris, also of the United States, third in 2 min 9.3 sec.

Afterwards Woodroffe said: 'Before the start I thought Carl and not Spitz would win. I was in the next lane to Carl, so I hung on to him. That's all there is to it.' A journalist asked the two Americans whether they had ever heard of Woodroffe before. Robie said: 'I hadn't heard of him until they made the predictions in *Sports Illustrated*.' Ferris said: 'I'd never heard of him.' It was certainly an unexpected silver medal, and a just reward for some very hard work over the last few months.

I spent the most enjoyable time of these three days at the women's gymnastics. If there is one personality of these myriad Games it is Vera Caslavska, the blonde twenty-six-year-old Czechoslovakian gymnast. In the last three days she has won four gold medals to add to the eighteen others that she has collected in Tokyo and in various world and European championships.

The number of medals is not really significant, for in gymnastics they are scattered like confetti. But her personality has made her the most dearly loved foreign athlete in Mexico City. On Wednesday night in the team championship (which also includes the overall individual championship) she was only given 9.60 marks (out of a possible ten) after a superlative performance on the balance beam. For ten minutes the packed crowd in the huge amphitheatre howled their derision at the judges and set up a chant of 'Ver . . . a, Ver . . . a'. Only when the judges changed the scoreboard to 9.80 (they said the original score had been an electronic error!) did the bedlam subside.

One cannot describe her performance—one can only marvel at how such a feminine figure can perform such acts of grace, strength and beauty. She won the overall title on Wednesday and then on Friday night also won the gold medals for the asymmetrical bars, the horse vault and the floor exercise—although this last medal was not an outright win. She tied with the beautiful black-haired Russian girl, Ludmilla Petrik.

The remaining individual gold medal on Friday night—for the balance beam—went to the nineteen-year-old Russian girl Natasha Kuchinskaya, who also has a vehement following amongst the Mexican men. Prettier than Caslavska, she is more careful, less aware of her following. When asked on Wednesday night whether she had agreed with the judges or with the crowd over some of the markings—especially of her rival Caslavska—she replied with a smile: 'I agreed with the crowd because the majority is always right!'

Not only do these girls perform beautiful, controlled movements, but they are also beautiful in themselves. Four out of the six members of the young Russian team would carry off the prizes in any Miss World contest.

17
'I'M NOT JUST A SILLY OLD BRICKLAYER'

My colleague Hugh McIlvanney takes over at this point to record the efforts of the British boxers.

The punches which won Christopher Finnegan a gold medal were thrown in the Arena Mexico, but he was not officially recognised as Britain's first Olympic boxing champion since 1956 until he had achieved a less public triumph several hours later in a restaurant called Chalet Suizo. Finnegan's experience, for which there were legitimate if mildly hilarious reasons, was merely one more indication of how complicated competition at the highest levels of sports, and above all in the Olympic Games, has become.

His victory in the middleweight division of an undistinguished tournament had been deserved, if nerve-rackingly narrow. He was a clear outsider when he went into the ring late on the last Saturday of the Games (just as some of his workmates at home were getting out of bed to do a little Sunday overtime on a Middlesex building site). And in the first round it seemed that he was being affected by the formidable aspect and reputation of his opponent in the final, Alexei Kiseliov, a large, ruggedly constructed Russian who looked no frailer than he did when he won the light-heavyweight silver medal in Tokyo.

Kiseliov was one of three southpaws the draw set against Finnegan, who thus found his own right lead much less of an asset than it usually is. The Russian began by charging in with flurries of hooks that were haphazardly aimed but ominously heavy and the Englishman closed up apprehensively. Finnegan's work as a bricklayer has given him a healthily ruddy complexion, but now his cheeks flushed unnaturally as he used his long arms to shield his ribs and swung his head away from the higher blows. He did emerge from worried defensiveness to land one stiff right, but lost the round decisively to aggression that was powerful without being at all inspired.

The second round supplied hints of the transformation we were to see in the third. Finnegan took a couple of heavy swings on the back of the head and allowed himself to be bullied around the ring rather too much. But he scored with one really punishing left cross and at last his brisk right jab began to work effectively. It was a notably close round and most scorecards made it even.

Finnegan, rarely a weak finisher, surprised even his greatest admirers with the exciting excellence of his performance in the last round. Kiseliov had started to tire in the second and now a hard, short left to the face had him clinging on breathlessly. The British boxer was driving his jab home regularly, moving in confidently behind the punch to give it jolting force. He is a thoughtful fighter, with a realistic awareness of his own strengths and weaknesses, and earlier in the contest he had circled carefully to his left to minimise the effects of the swings and hooks the Russian delivered with his left hand.

But by this stage Finnegan was happy to stand in close, sure that his own body punches and the occasional right hook to the head on the break would do more damage than anything his opponent could throw. Afterwards he told us that at this point he was muttering elatedly to himself: 'You've gone, you great bleedin' Russki, you've gone.'

The extent of Kiseliov's physical deterioration since the first round was made obvious each time the referee pulled the boxers apart. He stood with head down, nostrils flared, chest heaving, the image of a bull set up for the kill. Finnegan is not a spectacularly destructive fighter and there was no swift, clean execution (indeed the Russian struggled back to land a hefty, clubbing right at the last bell), but he won the round by a margin that outweighed his deficit in the opening three minutes.

Archie Tanner, the Australian referee, brought the two men into the centre of the ring to await the announcement of the judges' figures. When they came they seemed a remarkably just reflection of what we had seen. Scored according to a system of awarding twenty points to the winner of a round, and a proportionately smaller total to the loser, the five cards (with Kiseliov's scores first) showed these figures: 58—59, 58—59, 58—59, 59—58, 59—58. Finnegan had won by three votes to two, or by just one point.

But he had won, and in the interview room, amid the inevitable squabbles over the rights of television, radio and the Press, he told us what it meant to him: 'I feel I've done something different, that for once I'm not just a silly old bricklayer.'

With Len Mills, Chairman of the Amateur Boxing Association and manager of the British team, sitting beside him he could hardly be expected to give a firm declaration on the possibility of a professional career and, sure enough, he moved discreetly out of range of all questions on the subject. His only immediate plan, he confessed engagingly, was to go home 'and try to increase the family', which at present is limited to one five-year-old daughter.

When the interview was over, Finnegan assumed that he had nothing else to do but dandify himself a little and head for the celebration party which Len Mills had laid on at Chalet Suizo, about a mile and a half from the arena. However, he had reckoned without the complication I mentioned at the beginning of the chapter. Suddenly a doctor and two laboratory attendants materialised and requested a urine sample in accordance with the drug-test regulations imposed at the Olympics. Unfortunately, Finnegan found, as the hurdler David Hemery had found earlier in the Games, that he could make no significant contribution to their cause. Water taps were turned on, words of encouragement were whispered, drinks were gulped down, but nothing could induce the desired flow of co-operation from the fighter and eventually the doctor and his assistants picked up their little container and trooped off with the British boxers to an upstairs room in Chalet Suizo. There they sat, tense as expectant fathers, as the meal was eaten and, more relevantly, the toasts were drunk. As the minutes and then the hours went by with still no sign from Finnegan, their faces grew longer. Then at last, at twenty minutes to two in the morning, he leapt to his feet with a whoop of delight and announced that he was ready to oblige. The ritual was performed and Britain's last gold medallist of the Games was in official possession of his prize.

Finnegan has the sense of humour to appreciate that eccentric postscript to his success. When I talked to him the night before the finals he told me that his chance of becoming Britain's first gold medallist in boxing for twelve years was only one reason why he was happy to be in Mexico City rather than handling a hodful of bricks at home. 'I would sooner have a fight a day than have to get up and work every day,' he told me. 'At home I can have a fight a day anyway—with the missus. And I wouldn't go three rounds with her. I need the headguard for that. She don't worry about the Queensberry Rules. The head and the lot goes in.' He smiled at the wild picture he had painted. 'She's a champion. Just be sure and say I got her photo pinned above me bed and I'll be safe. And say I'm desperate to get home to see her and our daughter, which is true.'

We were speaking in one of the large, functional dining halls at the Olympic village. The number of athletes had dwindled as the Games neared their close, but a few score of them sat around in their national uniforms of tracksuit and training shoes. Finnegan stood out in a brown leather jerkin, striped shirt, blue jeans and suède boots. His home is in Iver, Buckinghamshire, but it is impossible to avoid identifying him with London—he has the repartee and sharpness of a Cockney.

He is tall (6 ft 1 in. in street shoes) and slim enough to go into the ring consistently half a stone under the middleweight limit of eleven stone eleven pounds. His fair hair is combed forward on top and allowed to spread down into shaped sideburns. The nose is not flattened or badly marked, although it bears fractionally to the right at the tip. He would not look out of place in a Western.

He has the temperament, too, to go out calmly to face a fateful confrontation, but the way he expressed his attitude to the final would not have sounded strange coming from the mouth of Gary Cooper in *High Noon*: 'The way I look at it, why should you worry out here, where you got a referee and doctors and surgeries all ready to take care of you if you get done up? When you really got to worry is if you're coming out of a boozer at home and they come at you with them bottles and iron bars. That way you can be left lying there bleeding to death. Compared with that this is a picnic. Mind you, you do feel a bit duberish each time you get in there.' Was being 'duberish' the same as being dubious? 'I always call it duberish. It sounds a better word for when you don't know how the old battle is going to be. You know how it is when you feel like you got no energy in you. You wonder how you're going to take the first whack on the chin. Then you stick a few out and it's all right. I've never really felt what you would call fear in the ring. Of course, I've never had a real good spanking but I imagine if you get one you are too busy trying to get out of the way of some of the stick to worry about whether you are afraid or not.'

The only time he had come remotely close to taking a spanking in the Olympic competition was in his semi-final with the American Negro Alfred Jones, and even there the danger was only momentary. Finnegan, who had earlier used his combination of agile footwork, long, fast right leads and occasional left crosses to take good victories over a Tanzanian, a German and a Yugoslav, began against Jones by boxing cautiously on the retreat.

He won the first round, in spite of being swung rather than punched on to a ring post for a standing count near the end of it, and when old cuts around the American's eyes began to open (without bleeding) in the second, Finnegan was encouraged to punch with far greater authority and established an appreciable lead. But it was the way he withstood Jones' desperate onslaught in the third that justified at least a moderate optimism about his prospects of defeating Kiseliov in the final.

Jones had been told by his corner before the last round that he needed a knock-out to win and he came out swinging wildly. Finnegan, noticeably less mobile than he had been earlier in the fight, was caught as his opponent literally jumped in with a big right in a neutral corner. Wisely, he closed and tried to hang on, but he was shaken out of the clinch and almost immediately the right staggered him again. As he took his second standing count, those who had questioned his competitiveness under extreme pressure winced in apprehension. But, though he was to admit subsequently that he did not know whether he had been down and could not remember how many counts he had taken, he came back bravely to dominate the last few seconds of the contest with impressive right jabs.

The verdict in his favour brought boos and whistles, but even by the accepted standards of boxing crowds, in which ignorance of the sport is always a bigger factor than objectivity, the daily audiences at the Arena Mexico were notably ill-informed. The only time they appeared to be sure of what was going on was when a Mexican boxer walked down the aisle. Then they chanted 'Mehico, Mehico'. All too often 'Medico, medico' would have been more appropriate.

Certainly Augustin Zaragoza, the Mexican who fell to Kiseliov in the semi-final, did not look too healthy when their meeting ended after 1 min and 40 sec of the first round. The Russian hit Zaragoza with huge upward-swinging lefts that seemed sufficiently powerful to knock over a brick wall. It was reassuring after that unnerving spectacle to find Finnegan still sanguine.

'I know I'll be giving him at least half a stone, but he'll be giving me a few years,' he said as he removed a substantial dinner. 'He's thirty and I'm twenty-four. I don't mind giving him a pound for each year.'

'I don't know why Chris isn't a heavyweight the way he eats,' said Charlie Kerr, the small former professional fighter from Glasgow, who was assistant trainer to the team. 'It's nothing for him to have three or four steaks at a sitting. I'm telling you, I'd rather keep his photograph than keep him.' Kerr, who was there to help David James, England's first national boxing coach, was the joker of the outfit. 'You've no idea the trouble I've had teaching these people to speak English,' he would say in a thick Clydeside accent. 'I've told Chris not to worry about the final. When this Russian breaks your jaw he does it cleanly. He's decent enough that way.'

The boxers presented Kerr with a massive wooden spoon bearing all their signatures. It was their tribute to the greatest stirrer they have known. In fact, his ribbing did much to maintain morale.

Finnegan insisted that his own spirits had been high all along. 'I had seen some of the other boys work, and I never saw anything that stuck out as spectacular. There were no Sugar Ray Robinsons about, nobody I reckoned was going to make a mess of me. I had a go at the old altitude and that and it didn't feel too bad. So I thought I could go in there, box a bit and show a few people they had underrated me.

'If you ask me if I enjoy it, all I can say is that if I'm boxing nice and cool and making the other geezer miss and making him look a clown, dancing around and popping away, then I'm living it. But if I'm taking a bit of stick there's no pleasure in that—I'm not a masochist. I wouldn't say I like smashing people's heads in, I just like making them miss, making them fall through the ropes and all that. Mind, I wouldn't lose any sleep over it if I hurt them a little.'

He calculates that he has had something like 120 fights since becoming a senior amateur at nineteen, the highlight prior to Mexico being his A.B.A. Championship in 1966. His first experience with boxing gloves was at the age of five. 'My older brother Terry was a good amateur. He took out a pro licence, but on the way to his first fight he bumped into a couple of mates and went on the booze. He got steamed up and never showed for the fight. That was his professional career.'

The younger Finnegan was rather more dedicated in approaching his Olympic challenge. His hard outdoor work gives him a basis of fitness ('It makes you a bit durable') and he reinforced it with an enthusiastic response to the modern methods of conditioning favoured by David James. Len Mills, who, in addition to being Chairman of the A.B.A., is Chairman of its Training Committee, had the vision to enlist James, a former Welsh amateur champion at light-heavyweight and a Loughborough-trained physical educationalist. James and Mills put the boxers through six week-end sessions of circuit, weight and interval training at Crystal Palace and organised professional sparring as part of the Olympic preparation.

'It was a lot different from the old routine where you met on the plane and if a boy was five pounds overweight you sawed a leg off,' says James, a personable, articulate Cheshire man of thirty-five. 'Under Len, too, we have set up a system of coaching qualifications. Most of the old sweats are the salt of the earth and we can learn from them, but some of the training methods in boxing are archaic. You should need more than a bent nose, some scar tissue and a towel to be a trainer.'

Chris Finnegan's freshness at the end of a taxing series of five fights was eloquent testimony to the value of the new, enlightened approach to the training of amateur boxers in Britain and he went out of his way afterwards to stress his debt to these modern methods: 'There is no doubt that the new training had a lot to do with the way things went for me. The strength is there when you want it. It's like being in a car and you put your toe down and the power is there.'

It was not lack of condition that prevented the other British boxers from making a memorable impact on the Games. Perhaps Johnny Cheshire was handicapped by the strain of making featherweight, but of the remainder only the welterweight, Alan Tottoh, who was still noticeably affected by a family bereavement, and Carter, the victim of a ludicrous injustice, did less well than expected. We have long accepted that only the chance flowering of truly exceptional natural talent can enable Britain to make a show in international amateur boxing against such as the U.S.S.R., the other East European countries and Cuba, where officially there are no professionals and actually there are scarcely any amateurs.

There must still be serious doubts about whether boxing has any place in the Games. Like football, it is a sport in which the highest standards, the best performers, are to be found among the professionals and that is probably enough to invalidate it as an Olympic event.

Certainly if boxing is to continue to be part of the Olympics it must be run more efficiently than it was in Tokyo or Mexico. For a start, there should be an eliminating competition such as there is in football. In Mexico 337 boxers from sixty-nine nations contested eleven divisions, providing 298 bouts. It amounted to sufficient concentrated fighting to make the Hundred Years War look like a minor tiff, and placed an unfair emphasis on strength and endurance at the expense of skill.

The other grave flaw in the organisation of the boxing in Mexico was one that has become almost inseparable from the Olympics: incompetent judging and refereeing. Too many of the officials are recruited for reasons that have more to do with sports politics than experience or ability and the conduct of some of them in the Arena Mexico would have been uproariously funny if it had not had such serious consequences for the boxers who came within their jurisdiction.

The worst decision of all affected a British boxer, bantamweight Mickey Carter, who was our principal hope for a medal. In his second-round bout Carter came up against the Russian Sokolov (who went on to win the gold medal). In the first round Carter was briefly knocked down, but he was up on his feet instantly, waiting for the compulsory count of eight to finish when the referee, a Japanese gentleman by the name of Hozumi Tanaka, inexplicably stopped the contest.

But, for all its defects and its aggravations, its generally poor quality and the mysterious exasperating proliferation of southpaws (they outnumbered orthodox boxers), the tournament did leave us with some marvellous memories. None will last longer than the picture of Jerzy Kulej, the reigning light-welterweight champion from Poland, boxing with superb control and economy and using every particle of his strength and ingenuity to defend his title against the fluent, brilliantly equipped Cuban Enrique Regueiferos. Kulej won a magnificent victory in an unforgettable contest, but Regueiferos, who at twenty is eight years younger, may yet be one of the great names of boxing.

Then, of course, there was Finnegan. Gus D'Amato, whose years in the professional game have dampened his enthusiasm so little that he was able to sit through every match in the Olympic programme, spoke for many of us when he said of the Englishman's achievement: 'Some fighters can have a tremendous amount of talent and yet do not excite you, because you are aware that they are not really giving out in the ring, they are holding back something of themselves. Others give of themselves and they are the fellows who lift you out of your seat. Finnegan is like that. From the beginning I went with that boy. Sure he has deficiencies, some of them big ones, but in that ring he took what he had and laid it on the line. He moved you.'

With a gold medal and that tribute as a bonus, Chris Finnegan is entitled to think that he is much more than 'a silly old bricklayer'.

18
THE END OF A LOVE AFFAIR

Saturday, October 26th

This is the end of a love affair. Every four years since the beginning of the 1950s I have renewed a brief, idealistic existence with this woman who transforms pure physical effort into an experience of spiritual beauty. Now she is a raddled old tart.

It is not her fault. The sceptical world has courted her too fiercely and the world, being materialistic, nationalistic and mean, has made her parade her sex in front of a panel of doctors, urinate into a bottle to make sure she has not been taking drugs, and breathe into a plastic tube to prove she is not drunk. To me and other romantics she is dying under this treatment.

As Ron Pickering, Lynn Davies's coach, and a man who has devoted his life to sport and recreation, says: 'I cannot see the Olympics surviving for more than another four games. It is bloody tragic.'

How can you explain that one is falling out of love. How can one rationalise the love itself. It is a chemistry that makes one believe, with utter faith, that the Olympics are something much greater than sport. They are an example of men and women of all colours, creeds and races living together in harmony, striving for that supreme excellence of body and mind.

The Olympics demand a commitment that can be conveyed only by an individual example. Les West is a joiner. He is twenty-four years old, he lives in Stoke-on-Trent and he is one of the greatest cyclists that Britain has ever produced. Two years ago he came second in the world championship road race on the Nurburgring circuit in Germany.

West, naturally, received many tempting offers to turn professional. He rejected them all because he had this dream of winning an Olympic title. You can be cynical and say that one large element of the dream was the knowledge that an Olympic title would immeasurably increase those professional offers—but I do not believe it was so. He gave up two years of good money to concentrate on one race in which he could prove, before the world, that he was the best.

And so on Wednesday morning at ten o'clock he set off with 162 other riders down the motorway that bypasses Mexico City to the west. They were to race for four and a half hours over 122 miles of road. After only ten miles West was in the leading group when he ran over a small piece of gravel and punctured. He took his bicycle to the side of the road and waited for the service vehicle. Rider after rider raced by, the good ones first, the indifferent next and then finally 'the camel drivers'. At last after two and a half minutes ('It seemed like ten,' he said) the service vehicle arrived and gave him a new bike. But one man, on his own, cannot catch up two and a half minutes or more on a class Olympic field and within a lap West, knowing the impossibility of his task, came into the pit. 'It's all been for buggerall,' he said.

And yet it was for something. He once was near to tasting what the Olympics are all about: 'I was pushed out of the Olympic Games in Tokyo because of a muddle over medical certificates after a leg injury. I have worked for this chance for four years, spending a lot of time and money preparing for this race. I have had four months off work this year and lost my pay for that time. I felt like crying when it happened. I sat there and watched them all come by.'

I do not suppose that he will try again. He has only just been married and must look to his future. Perhaps the professional offers will not be so good but he will take them, for he is a better cyclist than he is a joiner. Yet, throughout his life, he will know that for four years he has devoted himself to a dream which was an idealistic compound of rivalry and companionship.

It is so difficult to explain. But then it is not easy to expose the heart and the mind of a man. Let me give one personal experience. The facts of the first four-minute mile were that Chris Chataway and I had the task of pacing Bannister for three and a half laps so that he, relaxed behind us, could unleash that fantastic sprint which he drew, not from his physical strength, but from his nervous energy.

But to both of us it was not as simple as that. We confessed to each other afterwards that we had both dreamed of beating Bannister, of hanging on as he came past and then taking him in the finishing straight. It may sound farcical, but an athlete does not reason—he only believes in the impossible.

Twenty-four hours after it was all over, after Chris and I had 'died' the second our tasks were completed, leaving Bannister to go on alone, all three of us went for a walk over Harrow Hill as the light faded. There was in that hour or two a closeness, man to man, such as I had never experienced before or since. We had trained together and fought together. We had been rivals and one man had proved himself incomparably the best. Yet there was no resentment—just a sweet relish of the past, a companionship of the moment, and resolutions, idealistic all of them, for the future.

That, for the competitors, is part of the meaning of these four-yearly gatherings. Yet here, in Mexico City, one finds bitterness and resentment, exploitation and cynicism. The world is imposing its own materialistic standards on the Games and they cannot live in such an atmosphere. Who is to blame?

Before he left for Moscow on Wednesday, Gabriel Karobkov, the chief Russian coach, sat on a wooden chair in a bare room in the Olympic village and told me: 'Perhaps it is the modern way of life, the swift changes. Perhaps it is the Press and television turning it all into a battle of nations. Perhaps it is because everyone at home, in whatever country they live, thinks that their country must not lie behind.'

And so people search for ways of making their country's athletes better. Some of the members of the International Olympic Committee themselves cynically buck the rules which they have made about altitude training. Doctors and coaches and athletes chase after new products that will improve the performances.

In my own sport I see two threats—altitude and hormones. Most of us are sick and tired of the altitude question. The predictions were correct, altitude was decisive, these were, in the words of Jim Ryun, the 'Unfair Games'. There are a few men who still argue, who try to prove that it only affected four athletic events, but they are only trying to justify their stand before the Games when they made light of the problem.

I did not see any of them in the competitors' enclosure at the canoeing finals yesterday when little Barbara Mean, only eighteen years old, was brought out of the changing room some twenty minutes after she and Lesley Oliver had finished the 500 metres pairs event. She had been given oxygen, but still her face was drained of colour under her light tan. She was carried by her team-mates to a car and then taken to the Olympic village to be put to bed. And you just stand there helpless, the anger rising until you cry out at the stupidity of that decision taken five years ago by the I.O.C., amongst the roulette wheels of Baden-Baden.

Unfortunately, altitude is a potent factor which will remain in athletics for ever. We know now that if you train and live at altitude your performance, in all events which take over two minutes, will be improved. So the distance athlete of the future who aspires to a gold medal will have to uproot himself and take to the hills. Without doubt these Games have done more damage to the amateur cause, which the I.O.C. hold most precious, than any amount of payola.

Hormones are an even more potent threat. Now, if you want to get anywhere in the 'heavy' field events, you must take Dianabol or its new 'improved' version—Maxibol. Your weight will increase, your performance will improve and your testicles will waste away. Those are the short-term effects. The long-term effects are unknown.

So far there is no practical way of detecting whether a person is taking Dianabol. All one does know is that consensus of opinion amongst the athletes is that all those who won medals in the heavy events, with perhaps one exception, were taking some form of hormones. If these events are to survive another four years then some test must be found. At present the only practical suggestion is that every athlete should have an official weight chart and that any unnatural weight increase would be considered as sufficient proof that the athlete was taking Dianabol or one of the many other similar hormonal products. It would hardly be proof in a court of law but something must be done urgently to bring us back to sanity.

It is the only drug that has not been eradicated. Spot checks in all events have eliminated all chance of doping. It may take a little gilt off your efforts if, as Bill Toomey said: 'You've just run the fastest 400 metres of your life and this little bloke comes rushing up to you. You think he wants to congratulate you but he only wants a sample. And it is pretty difficult to give one when you're dehydrated.' Indeed, Doris Brown, the American 800 metres runner, was followed by a medical attendant for eight hours after her event before she could fill the jar!

There have been only two doping scandals and both minor. The Dutch seigneur to the cycling team was sent home pronto after he was discovered injecting vitamins and hormones into the Dutch cyclists. The second incident concerned alcohol—just as much of a drug as caffein or amphetamine.

One of the five events of the modern pentathlon comprises pistol-shooting—it is really snap-shooting at a target you only see for a very few seconds. In practice a good pentathlete can score in the 180s or 190s (out of 200). But in competition their nerves get so taut that their score can drop drastically to 140 or 150. About eight years ago the Australian pentathletes discovered that a bottle, preferably two bottles, of good Australian 'plonk' would leave you in a happy enough frame of mind to score in the 170s. Everyone else latched on to this brilliant idea, but it was ruined in Tokyo when one competitor was discovered drunk in charge of his loaded pistol!

So the Swedish president of the International Modern Pentathlon Federation introduced breathalysers and the limit was set at 0.40 milligrams per millilitre—exactly half the present British standard for driving. Unfortunately for the Swedes, two of their competitors (who together with the Swedish gold medallist had carried off the bronze medals in the team events) were found to be over the limit. One registered 0.45 (he was let off) but the other registered 0.75 ('I only had two bottles of beer,' he said!) and was disqualified. And that was the end of their bronze medals.

The I.O.C. have moved effectively against drugs. They must do the same against the undercover payola. I have already reported that the two German shoe firms Adidas and Puma were paying anything up to 7000 dollars to one athlete to ensure that he wore their particular brand of shoes. Then last week we had the Black Power demonstration on the rostrum by Carlos and

Smith. A lot of fuss was made about the raised fist in a black glove, but not so much notice was taken of the fact that in the other hand they each held a Puma shoe—idealism in one hand, commercialism in the other.

But they are not the only ones on the payola roundabout. There is at least one athlete in every significant team taking this money. Yet when Everett Barnes, acting director of the United States Olympic Committee, leaked to two American pressmen the news that he was after certain American athletes and would have their gold medals taken away, nobody was very surprised that the two athletes he named, Smith and Lee Evans, were both black and had both taken part in Black Power demonstrations.

The shoe payola must be stopped and it can be, quite easily. We had the same sort of row in Grenoble over skis. What difference is there between trade-marks on skis and trade-marks on shoes? The controlling bodies of all sports must specify that no sportsman shall enter any arena with any markings, other than national markings, on his clothes and equipment.

I am not even certain about the national markings. It is nationalism which has done most to bring about the rape of the Olympic ideals—nationalism which starts in the stadium at the opening ceremony, is fed to the world by television and which comes back here as this huge weight of responsibility on every team. They are no longer competing man to man. It is now nation versus nation, black versus white, communism versus capitalism.

For the first time in five Olympics I will not be sorry to see the Olympic flame die tomorrow evening. Since Melbourne in 1956, when a child suggested to the organising committee that all competitors should mix freely in one vast throng of humanity, the closing ceremony has been the poignant highlight of everything the Olympics stand for—the concept of man as one huge family, striving, failing, succeeding together.

Tomorrow night there will be no such throng, for the I.O.C., those idealists, have destroyed this ideal by decreeing that the athletes—only six from each country—shall march nation by nation. And with that final demonstration of nationalism we shall say farewell to the Mexicans. Much that has happened here has not been their fault. They have organised the Games better than those who expected chaos dared to hope; far worse than those of us who thought, wrongly, that the old image—of a sombrero muttering *mañana, mañana*—was a myth of the past.

No, the real fault lies with the I.O.C. They have lost touch with modern developments and are doing nothing to curb the excesses of the Games. Earlier today I was looking up a cutting to see what I said about Abebe Bikila's victory in 1960 and I found these sentences: 'The Games have got out of hand . . . they are just too big. It seems that Mr. Avery Brundage . . . thinks so too. On Thursday [and the date of that Thursday was September 8th, 1960!] he said: "The Games are getting too big and too expensive. The I.O.C. is seeking ways and means of cutting them down." ' I commented at the time: 'They had better do it quickly.'

Tonight Avery Brundage said substantially the same thing during his final press conference. But will anything happen before Munich in 1972? Is it any wonder that I now feel that the Olympic movement, this movement that I loved, is now a raddled old tart?

19
FAREWELL

Sunday evening, October 27th

Humanity has saved me from my depression. Whatever the I.O.C. decree, they cannot stop the youth of the world from mingling in one vast polyglot throng.

The flame, lit months ago by the sun in Greece, died tonight and as it died the athletes and the pink-skirted hostesses took over the stadium prancing and jiving around the track. They make it all worth while, make me still want to fight for the Olympic movement. Already I can feel my spirit stir with anticipation at the feats and the courage which we will be witness to in four years' time.

The 19th Olympiad is dead and I do not mourn its passing. The 20th Olympiad has already dawned. If we would only entrust its care to the youth of the world then peace and goodwill might reign in sport for the next four years.

The vast electric scoreboard which has recorded some fabulous feats, some artificial ones, now reads: 'MUNICH'.

MEXICO 1968
RESULTS

MEN'S ATHLETICS
Track Events

100 METRES
1. J. Hines (U.S.) 9.9sec
   (World and Olympic record)
2. L. Miller (Jamaica) 10.0 sec
3. C. Greene (U.S.) 10.0 sec
4. P. Montes (Cuba) 10.1 sec
5. R. Bambuck (France) 10.1 sec
6. M. Pender (U.S.) 10.1 sec
7. H. Jerome (Canada) 10.1 sec
8. J. Ravelomanantsoa (Madagascar) 10.2 sec

400 METRES
1. L. Evans (U.S.) 43.8 sec
   (World and Olympic record)
2. L. James (U.S.) 43.9 sec
3. R. Freeman (U.S.) 44.4 sec
4. A. Gakou (Senegal) 45.0 sec
5. M. Jellingshaus (West Germany) 45.3 sec
6. T. Bezabeth (Ethiopia) 45.4 sec
7. A. Badenski (Poland) 45.4 sec
8. A. Omolo (Uganda) 47.6 sec

1500 METRES
1. K. Keino (Kenya) 3 min 34.9 sec
   (Olympic record)
2. J. Ryun (U.S.) 3 min 37.8 sec
3. B. Tuemmler (West Germany) 3 min 39.0 sec
4. H. Norpoth (West Germany) 3 min 42.5 sec
5. J. Whetton (G.B.) 3 min 43.8 sec
6. J. Boxberger (France) 3 min 46.6 sec
7. H. Szardykowski (Poland) 3 min 46.6 sec
8. J. Odlozil (Czechoslovakia) 3 min 48.6 sec
9. T. von Ruden (U.S.) 3 min 49.2 sec

10,000 METRES
1. N. Temu (Kenya) 29 min 27.4 sec
2. M. Wolde (Ethiopia) 29 min 28 sec
3. M. Gammoudi (Tunisia) 29 min 34.2 sec
4. J. Martinez (Mexico) 29 min 35 sec
5. N. Sviridov (U.S.S.R.) 29 min 43.2 sec
6. R. Clarke (Australia) 29 min 44.8 sec
7. R. Hill (G.B.) 29 min 53.2 sec
8. W. Masresha (Ethiopia) 29 min 57.0 sec

200 METRES
1. T. Smith (U.S.) 19.8 sec
   (World and Olympic record)
2. P. Norman (Australia) 20.0 sec
3. J. Carlos (U.S.) 20.0 sec
4. E. Roberts (Trinidad) 20.3 sec
5. R. Bambuck (France) 20.5 sec
6. L. Questad (U.S.) 20.6 sec
7. M. Fray (Jamaica) 20.6 sec
8. J. Eigenherr (West Germany) 20.6 sec

800 METRES
1. R. Doubell (Australia) 1 min 44.3 sec
   (equalled official World record, new Olympic record)
2. W. Kiprugut (Kenya) 1 min 44.5 sec
3. T. Farrell (U.S.) 1 min 45.4 sec
4. W. Adams (West Germany) 1 min 45.8 sec
5. J. Plachy (Czechoslovakia) 1 min 45.9 sec
6. D. Fromm (East Germany) 1 min 46.2 sec
7. T. Saisi (Kenya) 1 min 47.5 sec
8. B. Cayenne (Trinidad and Tobago)
   1 min 54.3 sec

5000 METRES
1. M. Gammoudi (Tunisia) 14 min 05.0 sec
2. K. Keino (Kenya) 14 min 05.2 sec
3. N. Temu (Kenya) 14 min 06.4 sec
4 J. Martinez (Mexico) 14 min 10.8 sec
5. R. Clarke (Australia) 14 min 12.4 sec
6. W. Masresha (Ethiopia) 14 min 17.6 sec
7. N. Sviridov (U.S.S.R.) 14 min 18.4 sec
8. F. Deguefu (Ethiopia) 14 min 19.0 sec
9. J. Wadoux (France) 14 min 20.8 sec
10. R. Maddaford (N.Z.) 14 min 39.8 sec
11. R. Finlay (Canada) 14 min 45.0 sec
12. E. Puttemans (Belgium) 14 min 59.6 sec

3000 METRES STEEPLECHASE
1. A. Biwott (Kenya) 8 min 51 sec
2. B. Kogo (Kenya) 8 min 51.6 sec
3. G. Young (U.S.) 8 min 51.8 sec
4. K. O'Brien (Australia) 8 min 52 sec
5. A. Morozov (U.S.S.R.) 8 min 55.8 sec
6. J. Mihail (Bulgaria) 8 min 58.4 sec
7. G. Roelants (Belgium) 8 min 59.4 sec
8. A. Risa (Norway) 9 min 09 sec
9. J. P. Villain (France) 9 min 16.2 sec
10. B. Persson (Sweden) 9 min 20.6 sec
11. J. Alvarez (Spain) 9 min 24.6 sec
   (V. Kudinsky (U.S.S.R.) did not finish because of injury)

MARATHON
1. M. Wolde (Ethiopia) — 2 hr 20 min 26.4 sec
2. K. Kimihara (Japan) — 2 hr 23 min 31.0 sec
3. M. Ryan (N.Z.) — 2 hr 23 min 45.0 sec
4. I. Akcay (Turkey) — 2 hr 25 min 18.8 sec
5. W. Adcocks (G.B.) — 2 hr 25 min 33.0 sec
6. M. Gebru (Ethiopia) — 2 hr 27 min 16.8 sec
7. D. Clayton (Australia) — 2 hr 27 min 23.8 sec
8. T. Johnston (G.B.) — 2 hr 28 min 4.4 sec

4 × 400 METRES RELAY
1. U.S. — 2 min 56.1 sec
   (World and Olympic record)
2. Kenya — 2 min 59.6 sec
3. West Germany — 3 min 0.5 sec
4. Poland — 3 min 0.5 sec
5. G.B. — 3 min 01.2 sec
   (M. Winbolt-Lewis, C. Campbell, D. Hemery, J. Sherwood)
6. Trinidad and Tobago — 3 min 04.5 sec
7. Italy — 3 min 04.6 sec
8. France — 3 min 07.5 sec

4 × 100 METRES RELAY
1. U.S. — 38.2 sec
   (World and Olympic record)
2. Cuba — 38.3 sec
3. France — 38.4 sec
4. Jamaica — 38.4 sec
5. East Germany — 38.6 sec
6. West Germany — 38.7 sec
7. Italy — 39.2 sec
8. Poland — 39.2 sec

110 METRES HURDLES
1. W. Davenport (U.S.) — 13.3 sec
   (equals Olympic record)
2. E. Hall (U.S.) — 13.4 sec
3. E. Ottoz (Italy) — 13.4 sec
4. L. Coleman (U.S.) — 13.6 sec
5. W. Trzmiel (West Germany) — 13.6 sec
6. B. Forssander (Sweden) — 13.7 sec
7. M. Duriez (France) — 13.7 sec
8. P. Schoebel (France) — 14.0 sec

400 METRES HURDLES
1. D. Hemery (G.B.) — 48.1 sec
   (World and Olympic records)
2. G. Hennige (West Germany) — 49 sec
3. J. Sherwood (G.B.) — 49 sec
4. G. Vanderstock (U.S.) — 49 sec
5. V. Skomarokhov (U.S.S.R.) — 49.1 sec
6. R. Whitney (U.S.) — 49.2 sec
7. R. Schubert (West Germany) — 49.2 sec
8. R. Frinolli (Italy) — 50.1 sec

Field Events

HIGH JUMP
1. R. Fosbury (U.S.) — 7 ft 4¼ in
   (Olympic record)
2. E. Caruthers (U.S.) — 7 ft 3½ in
3. V. Gavrilov (U.S.S.R.) — 7 ft 2¾ in
4. V. Svortsov (U.S.S.R.) — 7 ft 1 in
5. R. Brown (U.S.) — 7 ft 0¼ in
6. G. Crosa (Italy) — 7 ft 0¼ in
6. G. Spielvogel (West Germany) — 7 ft 0¼ in

POLE VAULT
1. R. Seagren (U.S.) — 17 ft 8½ in
   (World and Olympic record)
2. C. Schiprowski (West Germany) — 17 ft 8½ in
3. W. Nordwig (East Germany) — 17 ft 8½ in
4. C. Papanikolaou (Greece) — 17 ft 6¾ in
5. J. Pennel (U.S.) — 17 ft 6¾ in
6. G. Bliznetsov (U.S.S.R.) — 17 ft 4¾ in
7. H. d'Encausse (France) — 17 ft 2¾ in
8. H. Engel (West Germany) — 17 ft 0¾ in
9. I. Sola (Spain) — 17 ft 0¾ in
10. K. Isaksson (Sweden) — 16 ft 10¼ in
13. M. Bull (G.B.) — 16 ft 5 in

LONG JUMP
1. R. Beamon (U.S.)   29 ft 2½ in
   (World and Olympic record)
2. K. Beer (East Germany)   26 ft 10½ in
3. R. Boston (U.S.)   26 ft 9¼ in
4. I. Ter-Ovanesyan (U.S.S.R.)   26 ft 7¾ in
5. T. Lepik (U.S.S.R.)   26 ft 6½ in
6. A. Crawley (Australia)   26 ft 3¾ in
7. J. Paul (France)   26 ft 1¼ in
8. A. Stalmach (Poland)   26 ft 0¼ in
9. L. Davies (G.B.)   26 ft 0¼ in

TRIPLE JUMP
1. V. Saneev (U.S.S.R.)   57 ft 0¾ in
   (World and Olympic record)
2. N. Prudencio (Brazil)   56 ft 8 in
3. G. Gentile (Italy)   56 ft 6 in
4. A. Walker (U.S.)   56 ft 2 in
5. N. Dudkin (U.S.S.R.)   56 ft 0¾ in
6. P. May (Australia)   55 ft 10 in
7. J. Schmidt (Poland)   55 ft 5 in
8. M. Dia (Senegal)   54 ft 10¾ in

SHOT-PUT
1. R. Matson (U.S.)   67 ft 4¾ in
2. G. Woods (U.S.)   66 ft 0¼ in
3. E. Guschin (U.S.S.R.)   65 ft 11 in
4. D. Hoffman (East Germany)   65 ft 7½ in
5. D. Maggard (U.S.)   63 ft 9 in
6. W. Komar (Poland)   63 ft 3 in
7. U. Grabe (East Germany)   62 ft 5¼ in
8. H. Birlenbach (West Germany)   61 ft 8¼ in
   Unplaced: J. Teale (G.B.)   61 ft 2¼ in

DISCUS-THROW
1. Al Oerter (U.S.)   212 ft 6½ in
   (Olympic record)
2. L. Milde (East Germany)   206 ft 11½ in
3. L. Danek (Czechoslovakia)   206 ft 5 in
4. M. Losch (East Germany)   203 ft 9½ in
5. J. Silvester (U.S.)   202 ft 7¾ in
6. G. Carlsen (U.S.)   195 ft 1 in
7. E. Piatkowski (Poland)   194 ft 10½ in
8. B. Bruch (Sweden)   194 ft 6 in

HAMMER-THROW
1. G. Zsivotzky (Hungary)   240 ft 8 in
   (Olympic record)
2. R. Klim (U.S.S.R.)   240 ft 5 in
3. Lovasz (Hungary)   228 ft 11 in
4. T. Sugawara (Japan)   228 ft 11 in
5. S. Eckschmidt (Hungary)   227 ft 10½ in
6. G. Kondrashov (U.S.S.R.)   226 ft 7½ in
7. R. Theimer (East Germany)   225 ft 10 in
8. H. Baumann (East Germany)   223 ft 11½ in

JAVELIN-THROW
1. J. Lusis (U.S.S.R.)   295 ft 7 in
   (Olympic record)
2. J. Kinnunen (Finland)   290 ft 7½ in
3. G. Kulcsar (Honduras)   285 ft 7½ in
4. W. Nikiciuc (Poland)   281 ft 2 in
5. M. Stolle (East Germany)   276 ft 11½ in
6. K. A. Nillsson (Sweden)   273 ft 10½ in
7. J. Sidlo (Poland)   264 ft 4½ in
8. U. Von Wartburg (Switzerland)   264 ft 3½ in
9. M. Muro (U.S.)   262 ft 8¾ in
10. W. Pektor (Austria)   253 ft 11¼ in
11. A. J. Torres (Cuba)   245 ft 8 in
12. H. Salomon (West Germany)   241 ft 1¼ in

DECATHLON
1. W. Toomey (U.S.)   8193 pts
   (Olympic record)
2. H. Walde (West Germany)   8111 pts
3. K. Bendlin (West Germany)   8064 pts
4. N. Avilon (U.S.S.R.)   7909 pts
5. J. Kirst (East Germany)   7861 pts
6. T. Waddell (U.S.)   7720 pts
13. C. Longe (G.B.)   7330 pts

20 KILOMETRES WALK
1. V. Golubnichiy (U.S.S.R.)   1 hr 33 min 58.4 sec
2. J. Pedraza (Mexico)   1 hr 34 min
3. N. Smaga (U.S.S.R.)   1 hr. 34 min 3.4 sec
4. R. Haluza (U.S.)   1 hr 35 min 0.2 sec
5. G. Sperling (East Germany)   1 hr 35 min 27.2 sec
6. O. Barch (U.S.S.R)   1 hr 36 min 16.8 sec
7. H. Reimann (East Germany)   1 hr 36 min 31.4 sec
8. S. Ingvarsson (Sweden)   1 hr 36 min 43.4 sec
9. L. Karaiosifoglu (Rumania)   1 hr 37 min 07.6 sec
10. P. Frenkel (East Germany)   1 hr 37 min 20.8 sec
11. A. Jones (G.B.)   1 hr 37 min 32.0 sec
12. P. Busca (Italy)   1 hr 37 min 32.0 sec

50 KILOMETRES WALK
1. C. Hohne (East Germany)   4 hr 20 min 13.6 sec
2. A. Kiss (Hungary)   4 hr 30 min 17 sec
3. L. Young (U.S.)   4 hr 31 min 55.4 sec
4. P. Selzer (East Germany)   4 hr 33 min 9.8 sec
5. S. E. Lindberg (Sweden)   4 hr 34 min 5 sec
6. V. Visini (Italy)   4 hr 36 min 33.2 sec
7. B. Eley (G.B.)   4 hr 37 min 32.2 sec
8. J. Pedraza (Mexico)   4 hr 37 min 51.4 sec
9. K. H. Merschenz (Canada)   4 hr 37 min 57.4 sec
10. G. Klopfer (U.S.)   4 hr 39 min 13.8 sec
18. S. Lightman (G.B.)   4 hr 52 min 20 sec

WOMEN'S ATHLETICS
Track Events

100 METRES
1. W. Tyus (U.S.)   11.0 sec
   (World and Olympic record)
2. B. Ferrell (U.S.)   11.1 sec
3. I. Szewinska (Poland)   11.1 sec
4. R. Boyle (Australia)   11.1 sec
5. M. Bailes (U.S.)   11.3 sec
6. D. Burge (Australia)   11.4 sec
7. C. Chi (Taiwan)   11.5 sec
8. M. Cobian (Cuba)   11.6 sec

200 METRES
1. I. Szewinska (Poland)   22.5 sec
   (World and Olympic record)
2. R. Boyle (Australia)   22.7 sec
3. J. Lamy (Australia)   22.8 sec
4. B. Ferrell (U.S.)   22.9 sec
5. N. Montandon (France)   23 sec
5. W. Tyus (U.S.)   23 sec
7. M. Bailes (U.S.)   23.1 sec
8. J. Stock (West Germany)   23.2 sec

400 METRES
1. C. Besson (France)   52 sec
   (equals Olympic record)
2. L. Board (G.B.)   52.1 sec
3. N. Pechenkina (U.S.S.R.)   52.2 sec
4. J. Simpson (U.S.)   52.2 sec
5. A. Penton (Cuba)   52.7 sec
6. J. Scott (U.S.)   52.7 sec
7. M. Henning (West Germany)   52.8 sec
8. H. van der Hoeven (Netherlands)   53 sec

800 METRES
1. M. Manning (U.S.)   2 min 0.9 sec
   (World and Olympic record)
2. I. Silai (Rumania)   2 min 2.5 sec
3. M. Gommers (Netherlands)   2 min 2.6 sec
4. S. Taylor (G.B.)   2 min 3.8 sec
5. D. Brown (U.S.)   2 min 3.9 sec
6. P. Lowe (G.B.)   2 min 4.2 sec
7. A. Hoffman (Canada)   2 min 6.8 sec
8. M. Dupureur (France)   2 min 8.2 sec

4×100 METRES RELAY
1. U.S.   42.8 sec
   (World and Olympic record)
2. Cuba   43.3 sec
3. U.S.S.R.   43.4 sec
4. Netherlands   43.4 sec
5. Australia   43.4 sec
6. West Germany   43.6 sec
7. G.B.   43.7 sec

80 METRES HURDLES
1. M. Caird (Australia)   10.3 sec
   (equals official World record; new Olympic record)
2. P. Kilborn (Australia)   10.4 sec
2. C. Chi (Taiwan)   10.4 sec
4. P. Van Wolvelaere (U.S.)   10.5 sec
5. K. Balzer   10.6 sec
6. D. Straszynska (Poland)   10.6 sec
7. E. Zebrowska (Poland)   10.6 sec
8. T. Talysheva (U.S.S.R.)   10.7 sec

Field Events

HIGH JUMP
1. M. Rezkova (Czechoslovakia) — 5 ft 11¾ in
2. A. Okorokova (U.S.S.R.) — 5 ft 11 in
3. V. Kozyr (U.S.S.R.) — 5 ft 11 in
4. L. Valentova (Czechoslovakia) — 5 ft 10 in
5. I. Schmidt (East Germany) — 5 ft 10 in
6. A. Maittova (Czechoslovakia) — 5 ft 10 in
13. B. Inkpen (G.B.) — 5 ft 6¼ in

LONG JUMP
1. V. Viscopoleanu (Rumania) — 22 ft 4½ in
   (World and Olympic record)
2. S. Sherwood (G.B.) — 21 ft 11 in
3. T. Talysheva (U.S.S.R.) — 21 ft 10¼ in
4. B. Wieczorek (East Germany) — 21 ft 3¼ in
5. M. Sarna (Poland) — 21 ft 2¼ in
6. I. Becker (West Germany) — 21 ft 1¼ in
7. B. Berthelsen (Norway) — 21 ft
8. H. Rosendahl (West Germany) — 21 ft

SHOT-PUT
1. M. Gummel (East Germany) — 64 ft 4 in
   (World and Olympic record)
2. M. Lange (East Germany) — 61 ft 7½ in
3. N. Chizhova (U.S.S.R.) — 59 ft 8¼ in
4. J. Lendval (Hungary) — 58 ft 4 in
5. R. Boy (East Germany) — 58 ft 1¾ in
6. I. Christova (Bulgaria) — 56 ft 7¼ in

DISCUS-THROW
1. L. Manoliu (Rumania) — 191 ft 2½ in
   (Olympic record)
2. L. Westerman (West Germany) — 189 ft 6 in
3. J. Kleiber (Hungary) — 180 ft 1½ in
4. A. Otto (East Germany) — 178 ft 5½ in
5. A. Popova (U.S.S.R.) — 175 ft 3 in
6. O. Connolly (U.S.) — 173 ft 9 in

JAVELIN-THROW
1. A. Nemeth (Hungary) — 198 ft 0½ in
2. M. Penes (Rumania) — 196 ft 7 in
3. E. Jenko (Austria) — 190 ft 5 in
4. M. Rudas (Hungary) — 184 ft 11½ in
5. D. Jaworska (Poland) — 183 ft 11 in
6. N. Urbancia (Yugoslavia) — 181 ft 10 in
7. A. Koloska (West Germany) — 181 ft 1¼ in
8. K. Launela (Finland) — 177 ft 0½ in

PENTATHLON
1. I. Becker (West Germany) — 5098 pts
2. L. Prokop (Austria) — 4966 pts
3. A. Toth (Hungary) — 4959 pts
4. V. Tikhomirova (U.S.S.R.) — 4927 pts
5. M. Bornholdt (U.S.) — 4890 pts
6. P. Winslow (U.S.) — 4877 pts
7. I. Bauer (East Germany) — 4849 pts
8. M. Antenen (Switzerland) — 4848 pts
9 M. Peters (G.B.) — 4803 pts
10. S. Scott (G.B.) — 4786 pts
16. A. Wilson (G.B.) — 4688 pts

MODERN PENTATHLON

Individual result
1. B. Ferm (Sweden) — 4964 pts
2. A. Balczo (Hungary) — 4953 pts
3. P. Lednev (U.S.S.R.) — 4795 pts
4. K. Kutschke (East Germany) — 4764 pts
5. B. Onishchenco (U.S.S.R.) — 4756 pts
6. L. Gueguen (France) — 4756 pts

Team result
1. Hungary — 14,325 pts
2. U.S.S.R. — 14,248 pts
3. Sweden (Disqualified) — 14,188 pts
4. France — 13,289 pts
5. U. S. — 13,280 pts
6. Finland — 13,238 pts
9. G.B. — 12,893 pts

ROWING

SINGLE SCULLS
1. J. Wienese (Netherlands)   7 min 47.8 sec
2. J. Meissner (West Germany)   7 min 52 sec
3. A. Demiddi (Argentina)   7 min 57.19 sec
4. J. van Blom (U.S.)   8 min 0.51 sec
5. A. Hill (East Germany)   8 min 6.09 sec
6. K. Dwan (G.B.)   8 min 13.76 sec

COXED PAIRS
1. Italy   8 min 4.81 sec
2. Netherlands   8 min 6.8 sec
3. Denmark   8 min 8.07 sec
4. East Germany   8 min 8.22 sec
5. U.S.   8 min 12.60 sec
6. West Germany   8 min 41.51 sec

COXED FOURS
1. New Zealand   6 min 45.62 sec
2. East Germany   6 min 48.2 sec
3. Switzerland   6 min 49.04 sec
4. Italy   6 min 49.54 sec
5. U.S.   6 min 51.41 sec
6. U.S.S.R.   7 min

DOUBLE SCULLS
1. U.S.S.R.   6 min 51.82 sec
2. Netherlands   6 min 52.8 sec
3. U.S.   6 min 54.21 sec
4. Bulgaria   6 min 58.48 sec
5. East Germany   7 min 4.92 sec
6. West Germany   7 min 12.2 sec

COXLESS PAIRS
1. East Germany   7 min 26.56 sec
2. U.S.   7 min 26.71 sec
3. Denmark   7 min 31.84 sec
4. Austria   7 min 46.79 sec
    Netherlands   did not finish

COXLESS FOURS
1. East Germany   6 min 39.18 sec
2. Hungary   6 min 41.64 sec
3. Italy   6 min 44.01 sec
4. Switzerland   6 min 45.78 sec
5. U.S.   6 min 47.7 sec
6. West Germany   7 min 08.22 sec

EIGHTS
1. West Germany   6 min 7 sec
2. Australia   6 min 7.98 sec
3. U.S.S.R.   6 min 9.11 sec
4. N.Z.   6 min 10.43 sec
5. Czechoslovakia   6 min 12.17 sec
6. U.S.   6 min 14.34 sec

WEIGHT-LIFTING

BANTAMWEIGHT
1. M. Nassiri (Iran)   809¾ lb
    (Olympic record)
2. I. Foldi (Hungary)   809¾ lb
3. H. Trebicki (Poland)   787¾ lb
9. P. Mackenzie (G.B.)   727 lb

LIGHTWEIGHT
1. W. Baszanowski (Poland)   958¾ lb
2. P. Jalayer (Iran)   931¼ lb
3. M. Zielinski (Poland)   925½ lb
4. N. Hatta (Japan)   920¼ lb
5. Shin Hee Won (South Korea)   914½ lb
6. J. Bagocs (Hungary)   909 lb

FEATHERWEIGHT
1. Y. Miyake (Japan)   865 lb
2. D. Shanidze (U.S.S.R.)   854 lb
3. Y. Miyake (Japan)   848½ lb

MIDDLEWEIGHT
1. V. Kurentsov (U.S.S.R.)   1046¾ lb
    (Olympic record)
2. M. Ohuchi (Japan)   1002¾ lb
3. K. Bakos (Hungary)   969¾ lb
4. R. Knipp (U.S.)   964 lb
5. C. Lee (South Korea)   964 lb
6. W. Dittrich (East Germany)   958¾ lb

LIGHT-HEAVYWEIGHT
1. B. Selitsky (U.S.S.R.)   1068¾ lb
   (Olympic record)
2. V. Beliaev (U.S.S.R.)   1068¾ lb
3. N. Ozimek (Poland)   1041¼ lb
4. G. Veres (Hungary)   1041¼ lb
5. K. Arnold (East Germany)   1030 lb
5. H. Zdrazila (Czechoslovakia)   1018 lb
14. M. Pearman (G.B.)   936 lb
18. P. Arthur (G.B.)   914¼ lb

HEAVYWEIGHT
1. L. Zhabotinsi (U.S S.R.)   1261 lb
2. S. Reding (Belgium)   1212¼ lb
3. J. Dube (U.S.)   1212¼ lb
4. M. Reiger (East Germany)   1173¾ lb
5. R. Mang (West Germany)   1157¼ lb
6. M. Lindroos (Finland)   1090¾ lb

MIDDLE-HEAVYWEIGHT
1. K. Kangasniemi (Finland)   1,140¼ lb
   (Olympic record)
2. Y. Talts (U.S.S.R.)   1,118 lb
3. M. Golab (Poland)   1,090¾ lb
4. B. Johansson (Sweden)   1,085¼ lb
5. J. Kailajarvi (Finland)   1,068¾ lb
6. A. Nemessany (Hungary)   1,063¼ lb

WRESTLING
Free-Style

FLYWEIGHT
1. S. Naata (Japan)
2. R. Sanders (U.S.)
3. S. Sukhbaatar (Mongolia)
4. N. Albarian (U.S.S.R.)
5. V. Grassi (Italy)
6. S. Kumar (India)

FEATHERWEIGHT
1. M. Kaneko (Japan)
2. E. Todorov (Bulgaria)
3. S. Seyedabassy (Iran)
4. N. Karipidid (Greece)
5. P. Coman (Rumania)
6. E. Tedeev (U.S.S.R.)

WELTERWEIGHT
1. M. Atalay (Turkey)
2. D. Robin (France)
3. D. Urev (Mongolia)
4. Ali-Mohammad Momeny (Iran)
5. T. Sasaki (Japan)
6. Y. Shakhmuradov (U.S.S.R.)

LIGHT-HEAVYWEIGHT
1. A. Ayuk (Turkey)
2. S. Lomidze (U.S.S.R.)
3. J. Csatari (Hungary)
4. S. Moustafov (Bulgaria)
5. B. Khorloogyn (Mongolia)
6. J. Lewis (U.S.)

BANTAMWEIGHT
1. Y. Uetake (Japan)
2. D. Behm (U.S.)
3. A. Gorgoni (Iran)
4. A. Aliev (U.S.S.R.)
5. I. Chavov (Bulgaria)
6. Z. Zedzicki (Poland)

LIGHTWEIGHT
1. A. Movahed (Iran)
2. E. Valtchev (Bulgaria)
3. S. Danzandarjaa (Mongolia)
4. W. Wells (U.S.)
5. Z. Beriashvili (U.S.S.R.)
6. U. Chand (India)

MIDDLEWEIGHT
1. B. Gurevich (U.S.S.R.)
2. M. Jigjid (Mongolia)
3. P. Gardjev (Bulgaria)
4. T. Peckham (U.S.)
5. H. Gursoi (Turkey)
6. P. Doring (East Germany)

HEAVYWEIGHT
1. A. Medved (U.S.S.R.)
2. O. Douraliev (Bulgaria)
3. W. Dietrich (West Germany)
4. S. Dtingu (Rumania)
5. L. Kristoff (U.S.)
6. A. Anvari (Iran)

YACHTING

DRAGON CLASS
1. U.S. — 6 pts
2. Denmark — 26.4 pts
3. East Germany — 32.7 pts
4. Canada — 64.1 pts
5. Australia — 65 pts
6. Sweden — 71.4 pts
14. G.B. — 101.7 pts

FINN CLASS
1. U.S.S.R. — 11.7 pts
2. Austria — 53.4 pts
3. Italy — 55.1 pts
4. Australia — 67 pts
5. Greece — 71 pts
6. Finland — 72 pts
22. G.B. — 129 pts

FLYING DUTCHMAN CLASS
1. G.B. — 3 pts
2. West Germany — 43.7 pts
3. Brazil — 48.4 pts
4. Australia — 49.1 pts
5. Norway — 52.4 pts
6. France — 68 pts

STAR CLASS
1. U.S. — 14.4 pts
2. Norway — 43.7 pts
3. Italy — 44.7 pts
4. Denmark — 50.4 pts
5. Bahamas — 63.4 pts
6. Australia — 68.7 pts
10 G.B. — 87 pts

5.5 METRES CLASS
1. Sweden — 8 pts
2. Switzerland — 32 pts
3. G.B. — 39.8 pts
4. West Germany — 47.4 pts
5. Italy — 51.1 pts
6. Canada — 68 pts

SHOOTING

CLAY PIGEON
1. R. Braithwaite (G.B.) — 198 pts
2. T. Garrigus (U.S.) — 196 pts
3. K. Czekalla (East Germany) — 196 pts
4. P. Senichec (U.S.S.R) — 196 pts
5. P. Candelo (France) — 195 pts
6. A. Smelczyski (Poland) — 195 pts

FREE PISTOL (50 Metres)
1. G. Kosykh (U.S.S.R.) — 562 pts
1. H. Mertel (West Germany) — 562 pts
   (Olympic record)
3. H. Vollmar (East Germany) — 560 pts
4. A. Vitarbo (U.S.) — 559 pts
5. P. Malek (Poland) — 556 pts
6. H. Arlet (East Germany) — 555 pts
7. N. Onate (Cuba) — 555 pts
8. N. Bratu (Rumania) — 554 pts
29. C. Sexton (G.B.) — 543 pts
62. M. Loader (G.B.) — 512 pts

SMALL-BORE RIFLE: PRONE (50 Metres)
1. J. Kurka (Czechoslovakia) — 598 pts
2. L. Hammeal (Hungary) — 598 pts
3. I. Ballinger (N.Z.) — 597 pts
4. N. Rotaru (Rumania) — 597 pts
5. J. Palin (G.B.) — 596 pts
6. J. Loret (France) — 596 pts
34. E. Salles (G.B.) — 590 pts

RAPID-FIRE PISTOL
1. J. Zapedzki (Poland) — 593 pts
2. M. Rosca (Rumania) — 591 pts
3. R. Suleimanov (U.S.S.R.) — 591 pts
4. C. During (East Germany) — 591 pts
5. E. Masurat (West Germany) — 590 pts
24. A. Clark (G.B.) — 581 pts
26. R. Hassell (G.B.) — 580 pts

FREE RIFLE (300 Metres)
1. G. Anderson (U.S.)   1157 pts
   (World and Olympic record)
2. V. Kornev (U.S.S.R.)   1151 pts
3. K. Muller (Switzerland)   1148 pts
4. S. Kveliashvili (U.S.S.R.)   1142 pts
5. E. Vogt (Switzerland)   1140 pts
6. H. Sommer (East Germany)   1140 pts

SMALL BORE RIFLE (50 Metres)
Shooting from three positions
1. B. Klinger (West Germany)   1157 pts
2. J. Writer (U.S.)   1156 pts
3. V. Parkhimovich (U.S.S.R.)   1154 pts
4. J. Foster (U.S.)   1153 pts
5. J. Gonzalez (Mexico)   1152 pts
6. G. Ovellette (Canada)   1151 pts
7. P. Kohnke (West Germany)   1151 pts
8. K. Muller (Switzerland)   1151 pts

SKEET-SHOOTING
1. E. Petrov (U.S.S.R.)   198 pts
2. R. Garagnani (Italy)   198 pts
3. K. Wirnhier (West Germany)   198 pts
4. Y. Tsuranov (U.S.S.R.)   196 pts
5. P. Gianella (Peru)   194 pts
6. N. Atalah (Chile)   194 pts
14. A. Bonnett (G.B.)   191 pts
26. C. Sephton (G.B.)   188 pts

CYCLING

1000 METRES TIME TRIAL
1. P. Trentin (France)   1 min 3.91 sec
   (World and Olympic record)
2. N. Fredborg (Denmark)   1 min 4.61 sec
3. J. Kierzkowski (Poland)   1 min 4.63 sec
4. G. Sartori (Italy)   1 min 4.65 sec
5. R. Gibbon (Trinidad and Tobago)
       1 min 4.66 sec

2000 METRES TANDEM
1. France (D. Morelon, P. Teentin)
2. Netherlands (J. Jansen, L. Loevesijn)
3. Belgium (D. Goens, R. van Lancker)
4. Italy (W. Gorini, L. Borghetti)

4000 METRES TEAM PURSUIT
1. Denmark   4 min 22.44 sec
2. West Germany   4 min 18.94 sec
3. Italy   4 min 18.35 sec
4. U.S.S.R.   4 min 33.39 sec

1000 METRES SPRINT
1. D. Morelon (France)
2. G. Turrini (Italy)
3. P. Trentin (France)
4. O. Pkhazadze (U.S.S.R.)

4000 METRES INDIVIDUAL PURSUIT
1. D. Ribillard (France)
2. M. Jensen (Denmark)
3. X. Kurmann (Switzerland)
4. J. Bylsma (Australia)

INDIVIDUAL ROAD RACE (121¾ miles)
1. P. Vianelli (Italy)   4 hr 41 min 25 sec
2. L. Mortensen (Denmark)   4 hr 42 min 49 sec
3. G. Pettersson (Sweden)   4 hr 43 min 15 sec
4. S. Abrahamian (France)   4 hr 43 min 36 sec
5. M. Pijnen (Netherlands)   4 hr 43 min 36 sec
6. J. P. Monsere (Belgium)   4 hr 43 min 51 sec
7. T. Pettersson (Sweden)   4 hr 43 min 58 sec
8. G. Bramucci (Italy)   4 hr 43 min 58 sec
9. M. Rodriguez (Colombia)
       4 hr 43 min 58 sec
10. M. Kegel (Poland)   4 hr 44 min
34. D. Rollinson (G.B.)   4 hr 47 min 58 sec
50. B. Jolly (G.B.)   4 hr 57 min 42 sec

100 KILOMETRES TEAM TIME TRIAL

1. Netherlands — 2 hr 7 min 49.06 sec
2. Sweden — 2 hr 9 min 26.6 sec
3. Italy — 2 hr 10 min 18.74 sec
4. Denmark — 2 hr 12 min 41.41 sec
5. Norway — 2 hr 14 min 32.80 sec
6. Poland — 2 hr 14 min 40.98 sec
7. Argentina — 2 hr 15 min 34.24 sec
8. West Germany — 2 hr 15 min 37.25 sec
9. U.S.S.R. — 2 hr 16 min 39.58 sec
10. Mexico — 2 hr 16 min
11. G.B. — 2 hr 16 min 38.6 sec
  (W. Bilsland, R. Cromale, P. Smith and E. Watson)

SWIMMING
Men

100 METRES FREE-STYLE

1. M. Wenden (Australia) — 52.2 sec (World and Olympic record)
2. K. Walsh (U.S.) — 52.8 sec
3. M. Spitz (U.S.) — 53 sec
4. R. McGregor (G.B.) — 53.5 sec
5. L. Ilichev (U.S.S.R.) — 53.8 sec
6. G. Kulikov (U.S.S.R.) — 53.8 sec
7. L. Nicoluo Yanuzzi (Argentina) — 53.9 sec
8. Z. Zorn (U.S.) — 53.9 sec

400 METRES FREE-STYLE

1. M. Burton (U.S.) — 4 min 9 sec (Olympic record)
2. R. Hutton (Canada) — 4 min 11.7 sec
3. A. Mosconi (France) — 4 min.13.3 sec
4. G. Brough (Australia) — 4 min 15.9 sec
5. G. White (Australia) — 4 min 16.7 sec
6. J. Nelson (U.S.) — 4 min 17.2 sec
7. H. Fassnacht (West Germany) — 4 min 18.1 sec
8. B. Berk (U.S.) — 4 min 26 sec

100 METRES BACKSTROKE

1. R. Matthes (East Germany) — 58.7 sec (Olympic record)
2. C. Hickcox (U.S.) — 1 min 2 sec
3. R. Mills (U.S.) — 1 min 0.5 sec
4. L Barbiere (U.S.) — 1 min 1.1 sec
5. J. Shaw (Canada) — 1 min 1.4 sec
6. R. Schoutsen (Netherlands) — 1 min 1.8 sec
7. R. Blechert (West Germany) — 1 min 1.9 sec
8. F. del Campo (Italy) — 1 min 2 sec

200 METRES FREE-STYLE

1. M. Wenden (Australia) — 1 min 55.2 sec (Olympic record)
2. D. Schollander (U.S.) — 1 min 55.8 sec
3. J. Nelson (U.S.) — 1 min 58.1 sec
4. R. Hutton (Canada) — 1 min 58.6 sec
5. A. Mosconi (France) — 1 min 59.1 sec
6. R. Windle (Australia) — 2 min 0.9 sec
7. S. Belits-Geiman (U.S.S.R.) — 2 min 1.5 sec

1500 METRES FREE-STYLE

1. M. Burton (U.S.) — 16 min 38.9 sec (Olympic record)
2. J. Kinsella (U.S.) — 16 min 57.3 sec
3. G. Brough (Australia) — 17 min 4.7 sec
4. G. White (Australia) — 17 min 8 sec
5. R. Hutton (Canada) — 17 min 15.6 sec
6. G. Evhevarria (Mexico) — 17 min 36.4 sec
7. J. Alanis (Mexico) — 17 min 46.6 sec
8. J. Nelson (U.S.) — 18 min 5.1 sec

200 METRES BACKSTROKE

1. R. Matthes (East Germany) — 2 min 9.6 sec (Olympic record)
2. M. Ivey (U.S.) — 2 min 10.6 sec
3. J. Horsley (U.S.) — 2 min 10.9 sec
4. G. Hill (U.S.) — 2 min 12.6 sec
5. S. Esteva (Spain) — 2 min 12.9 sec
6. L. Dobroskokin (U.S.S.R.) — 2 min 15.4 sec
7. J. Rother (East Germany) — 2 min 15.8 sec

100 METRES BREASTSTROKE

1. D. McKenzie (U.S.) — 1 min 7.7 sec
   (Olympic record)
2. V. Kosinsky (U.S.S.R.) — 1 min 8 sec
3. N. Pankin (U.S.S.R.) — 1 min 8 sec
4. J. Fiolo (Brazil) — 1 min 8.1 sec
5. E. Mikhailov (U.S.S.R.) — 1 min 8.4 sec
6. I. O'Brien (Australia) — 1 min 8.6 sec
7. A. Forelli Lopez (Argentina) — 1 min 8.7 sec
8. E. Henninger (East Germany) — 1 min 9.7 sec

200 METRES BREASTSTROKE

1. F. Munoz (Mexico) — 2 min 28.7 sec
2. V. Kosinsky (U.S.S.R.) — 2 min 29.2 sec
3. B. Job (U.S.) — 2 min 29.9 sec
4. N. Pankin (U.S.S.R.) — 2 min 30.3 sec
5. E. Mikhailov (U.S.S.R.) — 2 min 32.8 sec
6. E. Henninger (East Germany) — 2 min 33.2 sec
7. P. Long (U.S.) — 2 min 33.6 sec
8. O. Tsurumine (Japan) — 2 min 34.9 sec

100 METRES BUTTERFLY

1. D. Russell (U.S.) — 55.9 sec
   (Olympic record)
2. M. Spitz (U.S.) — 56.4 sec
3. R. Wales (U.S.) — 57.2 sec
4. V. Namshilov (U.S.S.R.) — 58.1 sec
5. S. Maruya (Japan) — 58.6 sec
6. Y. Suzdaltsev (U.S.S.R.) — 58.1 sec
7. L. Stocklas (West Germany) — 58.9 sec
8. R. Cusack (Australia) — 59.8 sec

200 METRES BUTTERFLY

1. C. Robie (U.S.) — 2 min 8.7 sec
2. M. Woodroffe (G.B.) — 2 min 9.0 sec
3. J. Ferris (U.S.) — 2 min 9.3 sec
4. V. Kuzmin (U.S.S.R.) — 2 min 10.6 sec
5. L. Feil (Sweden) — 2 min 10.9 sec
6. V. Meeuw (West Germany) — 2 min 11.5 sec
7. V. Sharygin (U.S.S.R.) — 2 min 11.9 sec
8. M. Spitz (U.S.) — 2 min 13.5 sec

200 METRES INDIVIDUAL MEDLEY

1. C. Hickcox (U.S.) — 2 min 12 sec
   (Olympic record)
2. G. Buckingham (U.S.) — 2 min 13 sec
3. J. Ferris (U.S.) — 2 min 13.3 sec
4. J. Bello (Peru) — 2 min 13.7 sec
5. G. Smith (Canada) — 2 min 15.9 sec
6. J. Gilchrist (Canada) — 2 min 16.6 sec
7. M. Holthaus (West Germany) — 2 min 16.8 sec
8. P. Lazar (Hungary) — 2 min 18.3 sec

400 METRES INDIVIDUAL MEDLEY

1. C. Hickcox (U.S.) — 4 min 48.4 sec
2. G. Hall (U.S.) — 4 min 48.7 sec
3. M. Holthaus (West Germany) — 4 min 51.4 sec
4. G. Buckingham (U.S.) — 4 min 51.4 sec
5. J. Gilchrist (Canada) — 4 min 56.7 sec
6. R. Merkel (West Germany) — 4 min 59.8 sec
7. A. Dunaev (U.S.S.R.) — 5 min 0.3 sec
8. R. Hernandez (Mexico) — 5 min 4.3 sec

4×100 METRES MEDLEY RELAY

1. U.S. — 3 min 54.9 sec
   (World and Olympic record)
2. East Germany — 3 min 57.5 sec
3. U.S.S.R. — 4 min 0.7 sec
4. Australia — 4 min 0.8 sec
5. Japan — 4 min 1.8 sec
6. West Germany — 4 min 5.4 sec
7. Canada — 4 min 7.3 sec
8. Spain — 4 min 8.8 sec

4×100 METRES FREE-STYLE RELAY

1. U.S. — 3 min 31.7 sec
   (World and Olympic record)
2. U.S.S.R. — 3 min 34.2 sec
3. Australia — 3 min 34.7 sec
4. G.B. — 3 min 38.4 sec
   (Turner, Hemrow, McGregor, Jarvis)
5. East Germany — 3 min 38.8 sec
6. West Germany — 3 min 39 sec

4×200 METRES FREE-STYLE RELAY

1. U.S. — 7 min 52.3 sec
2. Australia — 7 min 53.7 sec
3. U.S.S.R. — 8 min 1.6 sec
4. Canada — 8 min 3.2 sec
5. France — 8 min 3.7 sec
6. West Germany — 8 min 4.3 sec
7. East Germany — 8 min 6 sec
8. Sweden — 8 min 12.1 sec

SPRINGBOARD DIVING

1. B. Wrighton (U.S.) — 170.15 pts
2. K. Dibiasi (Italy) — 159.74 pts
3. J. Henry (U.S.) — 158.09 pts
4. L. Nino de Rivera (Mexico) — 155.71 pts
5. F. Cagnotto (Italy) — 155.70 pts
6. K. Russell (U.S.) — 151.75 pts

HIGHBOARD

1. K. Dibiasi (Italy)   164.18 pts
2. A. Gaxiola (Mexico)   154.49 pts
3. E. Young (U.S.)   153.93 pts
4. K. Russell (U.S.)   152.34 pts
5. J. Robinson (Mexico)   143.62 pts
6. L. Matthes (East Germany)   141.75 pts
7. L. Nino de Rivera (Mexico)   141.16 pts
8. F. Cagnotto (Italy)   138.89 pts
9. M. Safonov (U.S.S.R.)   138.77 pts
10. V. Vasin (U.S.S.R.)   138.40 pts
11. T. Anderson (Sweden)   131.21 pts
12. B. Wucherpfenning (West Germany)   129.49 pts

SWIMMING
Women

100 METRES FREE-STYLE

1. J. Henne (U.S.)   1 min
2. S. Pedersen (U.S.)   1 min 0.3 sec
3. L. Gustavson (U.S.)   1 min 0.3 sec
4. M. Lay (Canada)   1 min 0.5 sec
5. M. Gruner (East Germany)   1 min 1 sec
6. A. Jackson (G.B.)   1 min 1 sec
7. M. Segrt (Yugoslavia)   1 min 1.3 sec
8. J. Turoczi (Hungary)   1 min 1.8 sec

200 METRES FREE-STYLE

1. D. Meyer (U.S.)   2 min 10.5 sec
   (Olympic record)
2. J. Henne (U.S.)   2 min 11 sec
3. J. Barkman (U.S.)   2 min 11.2 sec
4. G. Wetzko (East Germany)   2 min 12.3 sec
5. M. Segrt (Yugoslavia)   2 min 13.3 sec
6. C. Mandonnaud (France)   2 min 14.9 sec
7. L. Bell (Australia)   2 min 15.1 sec
8. O. Kozicova (Czechoslovakia)   2 min 16 sec

400 METRES FREE-STYLE

1. D. Meyer (U.S.)   4 min 31.8 sec
   (Olympic record)
2. L. Gustavson (U.S.)   4 min 35.5 sec
3. K. Moras (Australia)   4 min 37 sec
4. P. Kruse (U.S.)   4 min 37.2 sec
5. G. Wetzko (East Germany)   4 min 40.2 sec
6. T. Ramirez (Mexico)   4 min 42.2 sec
7. A. Coughlaw (Canada)   4 min 51.9 sec
8. I. Morris (Sweden)   4 min 53.8 sec

800 METRES FREE-STYLE

1. D. Meyer (U.S.)   9 min 24.0 sec
   (Olympic record)
2. P. Kruse (U.S.)   9 min 35.71 sec
3. M. Ramirez (Mexico)   9 min 38.5 sec
4. K. Moras (Australia)   9 min 38.6 sec
5. P. Caretto (U.S.)   9 min 51.3 sec
6. A. Coughlaw (Canada)   9 min 56.4 sec
7. D. Langford (Australia)   9 min 56.7 sec
8. L. Vaca (Mexico)   10 min 2.5 sec

100 METRES BREASTSTROKE

1. D. Bjedov (Yugoslavia)   1 min 15.8 sec
   (Olympic record)
2. G. Prozumenshikova (U.S.S.R.)   1 min 1.9 sec
3. S. Wichman (U.S.)   1 min 16.1 sec
4. U. Frommater (West Germany)   1 min 16.2 sec
5. C. Ball (U.S.)   1 min 16.7 sec
6. K. Nakagawa (Japan)   1 min 17.0 sec
7. S. Baranina (U.S.S.R.)   1 min 17.2 sec
8. A. Norbis (Uruguay)   1 min 17.3 sec

200 METRES BREASTSTROKE

1. S. Wichman (U.S.)   2 min 44.4 sec
   (Olympic record)
2. D. Bjedov (Yugoslavia)   2 min 46.4 sec
3. G. Prozumenshikova (U.S.S.R.)   2 min 47 sec
4. A. Grebennikova (U.S.S.R.)   2 min 47.1 sec
5. C. Jamison (U.S.)   2 min 48.4 sec
6. S. Baranina (U.S.S.R.)   2 min 48.4 sec
7. C. Shibata (Japan)   2 min 51.9 sec
8. A. M. Norbis (Uruguay)   2 min 51.9 sec

100 METRES BUTTERFLY

1. L. McClements (Australia)   1 min 5.5 sec
2. E. Daniel (U.S.)   1 min 5.8 sec
3. S. Shields (U.S.)   1 min 6.2 sec
4. A. Kok (Netherlands)   1 min 6.2 sec
5. A. Gyarmau (Hungary)   1 min 6.8 sec
6. H. Hustede (West Germany)   1 min 6.9 sec
7. T. Hewitt (U.S.)   1 min 7.5 sec
6. H. Linder (East Germany)   1 min 7.6 sec

200 METRES BUTTERFLY

1. A. Kok (Netherlands)   2 min 24.7 sec
   (Olympic record)
2. H. Lindner (East Germany)   2 min 24.8 sec
3. E. Daniel (U.S.)   2 min 25.9 sec
4. T. Hewitt (U.S.)   2 min 26.2 sec
5. H. Hustede (West Germany)   2 min 27.9 sec
6. D. Giebel (U.S.)   2 min 31.7 sec
7. M. Auton (G.B.)   2 min 33.2 sec
8. Y. Fujii (Japan)   2 min 34.3 sec

100 METRES BACKSTROKE

1. K. Hall (U.S.)   1 min 6.2 sec
   (World and Olympic record)
2. E. Tanner (Canada)   1 min 6.7 sec
3. J. Swaggerty (U.S.)   1 min 8.1 sec
4. K. Moore (U.S.)   1 min 8.3 sec
5. A. Gyarmati (Hungary)   1 min 9.1 sec
6. L. Watson (Australia)   1 min 9.1 sec
7. S. Canet (France)   1 min 9.3 sec
8. G. Stirling (New Zealand)   1 min 10.6 sec

200 METRES INDIVIDUAL MEDLEY

1. C. Kolb (U.S.)   2 min 24.7 sec
   (Olympic record)
2. S. Pedersen (U.S.)   2 min 28.8 sec
3. J. Henne (U.S.)   2 min 31.4 sec
4. S. Steinbach (East Germany) 2 min 31.4 sec
5. Y. Nishigawa (Japan)   2 min 33.7 sec
6. M. Seydel (East Germany)   2 min 33.7 sec
7. L. Zakharova (U.S.S.R.)   2 min 37 sec
8. S. Ratcliffe (G.B.) Disqualified

4×100 METRES MEDLEY RELAY

1. U.S.   4 min 28.3 sec
   (World and Olympic record)
2. Australia   4 min 30 sec
3. West Germany   4 min 36.4 sec
4. U.S.S.R.   4 min 37 sec
5. East Germany   4 min 38 sec
6. G.B.   4 min 38.3 sec
   (Burrell, Auton, Harrison, Jackson)

SPRINGBOARD DIVING

1. S. Kossick (U.S.)   150.77 pts
2. T. Pogozheva (U.S.S.R.)   145.30 pts
3. V. O'Sullivan (U.S.)   145.23 pts
4. W. King (U.S.)   138.38 pts
5. I. Kramer (East Germany)   135.82 pts
6. V. Baklanova (U.S.S.R.)   132.31 pts
7. B. Boys (Canada)   130.31 pts
8. E. Anokhina (U.S.S.R.)   129.17 pts
12. K. Rowlatt (G.B.)   122.16 pts

200 METRES BACKSTROKE

1. P. Watson (U.S.)   2 min 24.8 sec
   (Olympic record)
2. E. Tanner (Canada)   2 min 27.4 sec
3. K. Hall (U.S.)   2 min 28.9 sec
4. L. Watson (Australia)   2 min 29.5 sec
5. W. Burrell (G.B.)   2 min 32.3 sec
6. D. Gasparak (Yugoslavia) 2 min 33.5 sec
7. M. Paz Corominas (Spain) 2 min 33.9 sec
8. B. Duprez (France)   2 min 36.6 sec

400 METRES INDIVIDUAL MEDLEY

1. C. Kolb (U.S.)   5 min 8.5 sec
   (Olympic record)
2. L. Vidali (U.S.)   5 min 22.2 sec
3. S. Steinbach (East Germany) 5 min 25.3 sec
4. S. Pedersen (U.S.)   5 min 25.8 sec
5. S. Ratcliffe (G.B.)   5 min 30.2 sec
6. M. Seydel (East Germany)   5 min 32 sec
7. T. Shipston (N. Z.)   5 min 34.6 sec
8. L. Vaca (Mexico)   5 min 37.3 sec

4×100 METRES FREE-STYLE RELAY

1. U.S.   4 min 2.5 sec
   (Olympic record)
2. East Germany   4 min 5.7 sec
3. Canada   4 min 7.2 sec
4. Australia   4 min 8.7 sec
5. Hungary   4 min 11 sec
6. Japan   4 min 13.6 sec
7. G.B.   4 min 18 sec
8. France (Disqualified)   4 min 15.4 sec

HIGHBOARD DIVING

1. M. Duchkova (Czechoslovakia) 109.59 pts
2. M. Lobanova (U.S.S.R.)   105.14 pts
3. A. Peterson (U.S.)   101.11 pts
4. B. Boys (Canada)   97.97 pts
5. B. Pietkiewicz (Poland)   95.28 pts
6. R. Krause (West Germany) 93.08 pts
12. M. Haswell (G.B.)   82.33 pts

WATER POLO

1. Yugoslavia
2. U.S.S.R.
3. Hungary
4. Italy
5. U.S.

6. East Germany
7. Netherlands
8. Cuba
9. Spain

WRESTLING
Greco-Roman

FLYWEIGHT
1. P. Kirov (Bulgaria)
2. V. Bakulin (U.S.S.R.)
3. M. Zeman (Czechoslovakia)

FEATHERWEIGHT
1. R. Rurua (U.S.S.R.)
2. H. Fujimoto (Japan)
3. S. Popescu (Rumania)

WELTERWEIGHT
1. R. Vester (East Germany)
2. D. Robin (France)
3. K. Bajko (Hungary)

LIGHT-HEAVYWEIGHT
1. B. Radev (Bulgaria)
2. N. Yakovenko (U.S.S.R.)
3. N. Martinescu (Rumania)

BANTAMWEIGHT
1. J. Varga (Hungary)
2. I. Baciu (Rumania)
3. I. Kochergin (U.S.S.R.)

LIGHTWEIGHT
1. M. Mumemura (Japan)
2. S. Horvat (Yugoslavia)
3. P. Galaktopoulos (Greece)

MIDDLEWEIGHT
1. L. Metz (East Germany)
2. V. Olenik (U.S.S.R.)
3. B. Simic (Yugoslavia)

HEAVYWEIGHT
1. I. Kozma (Hungary)
2. A. Roshin (U.S.S.R.)
3. P. Kment (Czechoslovakia)

BASKETBALL

1. U.S.
2. Yugoslavia
3. U.S.S.R.
4. Brazil

BOXING

LIGHT-FLYWEIGHT
1. F. Rodriguez (Venezuela)
2. Young-Ju Jee (South Korea)
3. H. Marbley (U.S.)
3. H. Skrzypezac (Poland)

BANTAMWEIGHT
1. V. Sokolov (U.S.S.R.)
2. E. Mukwanga (Uganda)
3. E. Moricka (Japan)
3. S. K. Chang (South Korea)

LIGHTWEIGHT
1. R. Harris (U.S.)
2. J. Grudzien (Poland)
3. C. Cutov (Rumania)
3. Z. Vujin (Yugoslavia)

FLYWEIGHT
1. R. Delgado (Mexico)
2. A. Olech (Poland)
3. S. de Oliviera (Brazil)
3. L. Rwabogo (Uganda)

FEATHERWEIGHT
1. A. Roldan (Mexico)
2. A. Robinson (U.S.)
3. P. Waruingi (Kenya)
3. I. Michaliou (Bulgaria)

LIGHT-WELTERWEIGHT
1. J. Kulej (Poland)
2. E. Regueiferos (Cuba)
3. A. Nilsson (Finland)
3. J. Wallington (U.S.)

WELTERWEIGHT
1. M. Wolke (East Germany)
2. J. Bessala (Cameroons)
3. V. Musalimov (U.S.S.R.)
3. M. Guilloti (Argentina)

MIDDLEWEIGHT
1. C. Finnegan (G.B.)
2. A. Kiselev (U.S.S.R.)
3. A. Zaragoza (Mexico)
3. A. Jones (U.S.)

LIGHT-MIDDLEWEIGHT
1. B. Lagutin (U.S.S.R.)
2. R. Garbey (Cuba)
3. J. Baldwin (U.S.)
3. G. Meyer (West Germany)

LIGHT- HEAVYWEIGHT
1. D. Pozniak (U.S.S.R.)
2. I. Monea (Rumania)
3. G. Stankov (Bulgaria)
3. S. Dragan (Poland)

HEAVYWEIGHT
1. G. Foreman (U.S.)
2. I. Chepulis (U.S.S.R.)
3. G. Bambini (Italy)
3. J. Rocha (Mexico)

CANOEING—MEN

KAYAK SINGLES—1000 METRES
1. M. Hesz (Hungary) — 4 min 2.63 sec
2. A. Shaparenko (U.S.S.R.) — 4 min 3.58 sec
3. E. Hansen (Denmark) — 4 min 4.39 sec
4. W. Szuszkiewicz (Poland) — 4 min 6.36 sec
5. R. Peterson (Sweden) — 4 min 7.86 sec
6. V. Mara (Czechoslovakia) — 4 min 9.35 sec
7. A. Contolenco (Rumania) — 4 min 9.96 sec
8. W. Lange (East Germany) — 4 min 10.03 sec
9. P. Hoekstra (Netherlands) — 4 min 13.28 sec

KAYAK FOURS—1000 METRES
1. Norway — 3 min 14.38 sec
2. Rumania — 3 min 14.5 sec
3. Hungary — 3 min 15 sec
4. Sweden — 3 min 16.68 sec
5. Finland — 3 min 17.28 sec
6. East Germany — 3 min 18.03 sec
7. Austria — 3 min 18.95 sec
8. Poland — 3 min 22.1 sec
9. Denmark — 3 min 25.64 sec

KAYAK PAIRS—1000 METRES
1. U.S.S.R. — 3 min 37.54 sec
2. Hungary — 3 min 38.44 sec
3. Austria — 3 min 40.71 sec
4. Netherlands — 3 min 41.36 sec
5. Sweden — 3 min 41.99 sec
6. Rumania — 3 min 45.18 sec
7. Belgium — 3 min 45.21 sec
8. Italy — 3 min 46.8 sec
9. West Germany — 4 min 2.98 sec

CANADIAN SINGLES—1000 METRES
1. T. Tatai (Hungary) — 4 min 36.14 sec
2. D. Lewe (West Germany) — 4 min 38.31 sec
3. V. Galkov (U.S.S.R.) — 4 min 40.42 sec
4. J. Ctvrtecka (Czechoslovakia) — 4 min 40.74 sec
5. B. Lubenov (Bulgaria) — 4 min 43.43 sec
6. O. Emanuelsson (Sweden) — 4 min 45.8 sec
7. I. Patzaichin (Rumania) — 4 min 49.32 sec
8. A. Weigand (U.S.) — 4 min 50.42 sec
9. C. Hook (Canada) — 4 min 55.88 sec

CANADIAN PAIRS—1000 METRES
1. Rumania — 4 min 7.18 sec
2. Hungary — 4 min 8.77 sec
3. U.S.S.R. — 4 min 11.30 sec
4. Mexico — 4 min 15.24 sec
5. Sweden — 4 min 16.6 sec
6. East Germany — 4 min 26.36 sec
7. West Germany — 4 min 26.36 sec
8. Bulgaria — 4 min 26.74 sec
Czechoslovakia disqualified

CANOEING—WOMEN

KAYAK SINGLES—500 METRES
1. L. Pinaeva (U.S.S.R.) 2 min 11.9 sec
2. R. Breuer (West Germany) 2 min 12.71 sec
3. V. Dumitru (Rumania) 2 min 13.22 sec
4. M. Smoke (U.S.) 2 min 14.68 sec
5. P. Vavrova (Czechoslovakia) 2 min 14.78 sec
6. A. Nussner (East Germany) 2 min 16.2 sec
7. I. M. Svensson (Sweden) 2 min 16.4 sec
8. M. Jaapies (Netherlands) 2 min 18.38 sec
9. A. Pfeffer (Hungary) did not finish.

KAYAK PAIRS—500 METRES
1. West Germany 1 min 56.4 sec
2. Hungary 1 min 58.6 sec
3. U.S.S.R. 1 min 58.16 sec
4. Rumania 1 min 59.17 sec
5. East Germany 2 min 0.18 sec
6. Netherlands 2 min 2.06 sec
7. U.S. 2 min 2.97 sec
8. G.B. 2 min 3.7 sec
   (L. Oliver and B. Mean)
9. Poland 2 min 4.2 sec

EQUESTRIAN

INDIVIDUAL JUMPING GRAND PRIX DES NATIONS
1. W. Steinkraus (U.S.) (Snowbound) 4 faults
2. M. Coakes (G.B.) (Stroller) 8
3. D. Broome (G.B.) (Mister Softee) 12
4. F. D. Chapot (U.S.) (San Lucas) 12
5. H. G. Winkler (West Germany) (Enigk) 12
6. J. Elder (Canada) (The Immigrant) 12

INDIVIDUAL GRAND PRIX DE DRESSAGE
1. I. Kizimov (U.S.S.R.) (Ijor) 1572 pts
2. J. Neckermann (West Germany) (Marino) 1546 pts
3. R. Klimke (West Germany) (Dux) 1537 pts
4. I. Kalita (U.S.S.R.) (Absent) 1519 pts
5. H. Koehler (East Germany) (Neuschnee) 1475 pts
6. E. Petushkova (U.S.S.R.) (Pepel) 1471 pts
7. G. Fisher (Switzerland) (Wald) 1465 pts

TEAM GRAND PRIX DE DRESSAGE
1. West Germany 2699 pts
2. U.S.S.R. 2657 pts
3. Switzerland 2547 pts
4. East Germany 2357 pts
5. G.B. 2332 pts
   (L. Johnstone, J. Hall D. Lawrence)

TEAM JUMPING GRAND PRIX DES NATIONS
1. Canada 102.75 pen pts
2. France 110.5 pen pts
3. West Germany 117.25 pen pts
4. U.S. 117.5 pen pts
5. Italy 129.25 pen pts
6. Switzerland 136.75 pen pts

THREE-DAY EVENT (INDIVIDUAL)
1. J. J. Guyon (France) (Pitou) 38.86 pen pts
2. D. Allhusen (G.B.) (Lochinvar) 41.61 pen pts
3. M. Page (U.S.) (Foster) 52.31 pen pts
4. R. Meade (G.B.) (Cornishman) 64.46 pen pts
5. B. Jones (G.B.) 69.86 pen pts
   (The Poacher)
6. J. Wofford (U.S.) (Kilkenny) 74.06 pen pts
7. J. Jobling Purser (Italy) 79.11 pen pts
   (Jenny)

THREE-DAY EVENT (TEAM)
1. G.B. 175.93 pen pts
2. U.S. 245.87 pen pts
3. Australia 331.26 pen pts
4. France 505.83 pen pts
5. West Germany 518.22 pen pts
6. Mexico 631.56 pen pts

FENCING

MEN'S INDIVIDUAL FOIL
1. I. Drimba (Rumania) 4 wins 1 defeat
2. J. Kamuti (Hungary) 3 wins 2 defeats (14 touches)
3. D. Revenu (France) 3 wins 2 defeats (17 touches)
4. C. Noel (France) 2 wins 3 defeats (18 touches)
5. J. Magnan (France) 2 wins 3 defeats (22 touches)
6. M. Tiu (Rumania) 1 win 4 defeats

WOMEN'S INDIVIDUAL FOIL
1. E. Novikova (U.S.S.R.) 4 wins 1 defeat
2. P. Roldan (Mexico) 3 wins 2 defeats
3. I. Rejto (Hungary) 3 wins 2 defeats
4. B. Gapais (France) 2 wins 3 defeats
5. K. Palm (Sweden) 2 wins 3 defeats
6. G. Gorokhova (U.S.S.R.) 1 win 4 defeats

MEN'S INDIVIDUAL ÉPÉE
1. G. Kulcsar (Hungary) — 4 wins 1 defeat (after barrage)
2. G. Kriss (U.S.S.R.) — 4 wins 1 defeat (after barrage)
3. G. Saccaro (Italy) — 4 wins 1 defeat (after barrage)
4. V. Mondzolevski (U.S.S.R.) — 2 wins 3 defeats
5. H. Polzhuber (Austria) — 1 win 4 defeats
6. J. P. Allmand (France) — 0 wins 5 defeats

MEN'S TEAM FOIL
1. France
2. U.S.S.R.
3. Poland
4. Rumania
5. Hungary
6. West Germany

MEN'S TEAM ÉPÉE
1. Hungary
2. U.S.S.R.
3. Poland
4. West Germany
5. East Germany
6. Italy

MEN'S INDIVIDUAL SABRE
1. J. Pawlowski (Poland) — 4 wins 1 defeat
2. M. Rakita (U.S.S.R.) — 4 wins 1 defeat
3. T. Pezsa (Hungary) — 3 wins 2 defeats
4. V. Nazlimov (U.S.S.R.) — 3 wins 2 defeats
5. R. Rigoli (Italy) — 1 win 4 defeats
6. J. Ntwara (Poland) — 0 wins 5 defeats

WOMEN'S TEAM FOIL
1. U.S.S.R.
2. Hungary
3. Rumania
4. France
5. West Germany
6. Italy

MEN'S TEAM SABRE
1. U.S.S.R.
2. Italy
3. Hungary
4. France
5. Poland
6. U.S.

GYMNASTICS—MEN

FLOOR EXERCISES
1. S. Kato (Japan) — 19.475 pts
2. A. Nakayama (Japan) — 19.4 pts
3. T. Kato (Japan) — 19.275 pts
4. M. Tsukahara (Japan) — 19.05 pts
5. V. Karasev (U.S.S.R.) — 18.95 pts
6. E. Kenmotsu (Japan) — 18.925 pts

RINGS
1. A. Nakayama (Japan) — 19.45 pts
2. M. Voronin (U.S.S.R.) — 19.325 pts
3. S. Kato (Japan) — 19.225 pts
3. M. Tsukahara (Japan) — 19.125 pts
5. T. Kato (Japan) — 19.05 pts
6. S. Diomidov (U.S.S.R.) — 18.975 pts

PARALLEL BARS
1. A. Nakayama (Japan) — 19.475 pts
2. N. Voronin (U.S.S.R.) — 19.425 pts
3. Y. Klimenko (U.S.S.R.) — 19.225 pts
4. T. Kato (Japan) — 19.2 pts
4. E. Kenmotsu (Japan) — 19.175 pts

HORIZONTAL BAR
1. M. Voronin (U.S.S.R.) — 19.55 pts
1. A. Nakayama (Japan) — 19.55 pts
3. E. Kenmotsu (Japan) — 19.375 pts
4. K. Koste (East Germany) — 19.225 pts
5. S. Diomodov (U.S.S.R.) — 19.15 pts
6. Y. Endo (Japan) — 19.025 pts

HORSE VAULT
1. M. Voronin (U.S.S.R.) — 19 pts
2. Y. Endo (Japan) — 18.95 pts
3. S. Diomodov (U.S.S.R.) — 18.925 pts
4. T. Kato (Japan) — 18.775 pts
5. A. Nakayama (Japan) — 18.725 pts
6. E. Kenmotsu (Japan) — 18.65 pts

POMMELLED HORSE
1. M. Cerar (Yugoslavia) — 19.325 pts
2. O. Laiho (Finland) — 19.225 pts
3. M. Voronin (U.S.S.R.) — 19.2 pts
4. W. Kubica (Poland) — 19.15 pts
5. E. Kenmotsu (Japan) — 19.05 pts
6. V. Klimenko (U.S.S.R.) — 18.95 pts

COMBINED INDIVIDUAL EXERCISES
1. S. Kato (Japan) — 115.9 pts
2. M. Voronin (U.S.S.R.) — 115.85 pts
3. A. Nakayama (Japan) — 115.65 pts
4. E. Kenmotsu (Japan) — 114.9 pts
5. T. Kato (Japan) — 114.85 pts
6. S. Diomidov (U.S.S.R.) — 114.1 pts
79. S. Wild (G.B.) — 105.5 pts
91. M. Booth (G.B.) — 103.65 pts

MEN'S TEAM CHAMPIONSHIP
1. Japan — 575.9 pts
2. U.S.S.R. — 571.1 pts
3. East Germany — 557.15 pts
4. Czechoslovakia — 557.1 pts
5. Poland — 555.4 pts
6. Yugoslavia — 550.75 pts

GYMNASTICS—WOMEN

BEAM
1. N. Kuchinskaya (U.S.S.R.) — 19.65 pts
2. V. Caslavska (Czechoslovakia) — 19.575 pts
3. L. Petrik (U.S.S.R.) — 19.25 pts
4. L. Metheny (U.S.) — 19.225 pts
. K. Janz (East Germany) — 19.225 pts
6. E. Zuchold (East Germany) — 19.15 pts

FLOOR EXERCISES
1. L. Petik (U.S.S.R.) — 19.675 pts
2. V. Caslavska (Czechoslovakia) — 19.675 pts
3. N. Kuchinskaya (U.S.S.R.) — 19.65 pts
4. Z. Voronina (U.S.S.R.) — 19.55 pts
5. K. O. Karaseva (U.S.S.R.) — 19.325 pts
5. B. Rimnacova (Czechoslovakia) — 19.325 pts

ASYMMETRICAL BARS
1. V. Caslavska (Czechoslovakia) — 19.65 pts
2. K. Janz (East Germany) — 19.5 pts
3. Z. Voronina (U.S.S.R.) — 19.425 pts
4. B. Rimnacova (Czechoslovakia) — 19.35 pts
5. E. Zuchold (East Germany) — 19.325 pts
6. M. Sklenickova (Czechoslovakia) — 18.2 pts

HORSE VAULT
1. V. Caslavska (Czechoslovakia) — 19.775 pts
2. E. Zuchold (East Germany) — 19.625 pts
3. Z. Voronina (U.S.S.R.) — 19.5 pts
4. M. Krajcirova (Czechoslovakia) — 19.475 pts
5. N. Kuchinskaya (U.S.S.R.) — 19.325 pts
5. M. Sklenickova (Czechoslovakia) — 19.325 pts

COMBINED INDIVIDUAL EXERCISES
1. V. Caslavska (Czechoslovakia) — 78.25 pts
2. Z. Voronina (U.S.S.R.) — 76.85 pts
3. N. Kuchinskaya (U.S.S.R.) — 76.75 pts
4. L. Petrik (U.S.S.R.) — 76.7 pts
4 E. Zuchold (East Germany) — 76.7 pts
6. K. Janz (East Germany) — 76.55 pts
74 M. Bell (G.B.) — 67.95 pts
88. M. Prestige (G.B.) — 65.6 pts

WOMEN'S TEAM CHAMPIONSHIP
1. U.S.S.R. — 382.85 pts
2. Czechoslovakia — 382.20 pts
3. East Germany — 379.1 pts
4. Japan — 375.45 pts
5. Hungary — 369.8 pts
6. U.S. — 369.75 pts

HOCKEY

1. Pakistan
2. Australia
3. India
4. West Germany
5. Netherlands
6. Spain
7. N.Z.
8. Kenya

SOCCER

1. Hungary
2. Bulgaria
3. Japan
4. Mexico

VOLLEYBALL—MEN

1. U.S.S.R.
2. Japan
3. Czechoslovakia
4. East Germany

VOLLEYBALL—WOMEN

1. U.S.S.R.
2. Japan
3. Poland
4. Peru

OLYMPIC MEDALS TABLE

	Gold	Silver	Bronze	Total		Gold	Silver	Bronze	Total
U.S.	45	27	34	106	Canada	1	3	1	5
U.S.S.R.	29	32	30	91	Finland	1	2	1	4
Japan	11	7	7	25	Ethiopia	1	1	0	2
Hungary	10	10	12	32	Norway	1	1	0	2
East Germany	9	9	7	25	New Zealand	1	0	2	3
France	7	3	5	15	Tunisia	1	0	1	2
Czechoslovakia	7	2	4	13	Pakistan	1	0	0	1
West Germany	5	10	10	25	Venezuela	1	0	0	1
Australia	5	7	5	17	Cuba	0	4	0	4
Great Britain	5	5	3	13	Austria	0	2	2	4
Poland	5	2	11	18	Switzerland	0	1	4	5
Rumania	4	6	5	15	Mongolia	0	1	3	4
Italy	3	4	9	16	Brazil	0	1	2	3
Kenya	3	4	2	9	Belgium	0	1	1	2
Mexico	3	3	3	9	Uganda	0	1	1	2
Yugoslavia	3	3	2	8	South Korea	0	1	1	2
Holland	3	3	1	7	Cameroons	0	1	0	1
Bulgaria	2	4	3	9	Jamaica	0	1	0	1
Iran	2	1	2	5	Argentina	0	0	2	2
Sweden	2	1	1	4	Greece	0	0	1	1
Turkey	2	0	0	2	India	0	0	1	1
Denmark	1	4	3	8	Taiwan	0	0	1	1